WHITEMETAL LOCOS
A KITBUILDER'S GUIDE
By IAIN RICE

WILD SWAN PUBLICATIONS LTD.

Thanks are due to many people for their help in producing this book, but I'm particularly indebted to Dave Ellis of South Eastern Finecast for letting me loose in his factory, and to Alan Ketley for the loan of so many splendid models.

Iain A. Rice

The photographs of Alan Ketley's engines are taken by **RAY PLASSARD** and **TREVOR BAILEY**. Unless otherwise credited, the remainder are taken by the author, **BARRY NORMAN** and **TONY SMITH**.

Designed by Paul Karau
Printed by Amadeus Press, Huddersfield

Published by
WILD SWAN PUBLICATIONS LIMITED
1-3 Hagbourne Road, Didcot, Oxon OX11 8DP

INTRODUCTION

No. 68616 — just another Finecast 'Buckjumper' in a long line? Not quite, for this model was built from the first set of castings for the revised kit, making it the very first of a new generation of 'Buckjumpers'.

The whitemetal locomotive kit was born in 1957, in the nether regions of Willesden, North London. As I started work on this book, it passed its thirtieth birthday, so it may be presumed to have reached some sort of maturity.

Although that pioneering kit, the K's GWR 14XX, is no longer in production, the second oldest example, the Finecast 'Buckjumper', is. However, not long since, I was charged with the task of reworking this veteran, to bring it into line with the latest productions in the genre. The work needed was a telling commentary on the development — or lack of it — that has gone into the whitemetal locomotive kit in the interim.

The Finecast 'Buckjumper', dating from June 1958, was found to need a certain amount of cosmetic work on the body. The footplate clearances needed adjustment for EM and P4, not really a consideration in 1958; several parts were added to enable more versions of the engine to be modelled; and a new, etched-brass chassis was provided, in place of the original cast block. Well, photo-etching still lay fifteen years in the future when the 'Buck' was born. Some new instructions were written — and that was it.

Is this to be taken, then, as an indication that no worthwhile progress has occurred in thirty years, that a whitemetal engine on a modern, finescale, 'state-of-the-art' layout is as anachronistic as a pony-trap on a motorway? Not a bit of it! What it really tells us is that the whitemetal locomotive, even in its infancy, was a very sophisticated, practical and worthwhile solution to the problem of producing relatively small numbers of high-quality models at a realistic price.

It was in the 1960s that the whitemetal locomotive kit really 'caught on', and the species mushroomed in all directions. By the end of the next decade, there were literally hundreds of different kits, from dozens of manufacturers, in production. Over this period, the growth in the choice and quality of ready-to-run models had changed the emphasis of the kit manufacturers from providing simple, rather basic models designed around off-the-shelf proprietary mechanisms to highly-sophisticated, fully-detailed and very complete models capable of being built into miniatures that only the most talented of scratchbuilders could hope to equal.

Today, the range of whitemetal loco kits has declined somewhat from its peak in the late 1970s. Several ranges have disappeared altogether, including the pioneering K's kits. Others have seen older, less satisfactory models deleted, while a more recent phenomenon has been the production of 'limited run' kits, which are not kept in production. Finecast, the other pioneering firm, recently changed hands, and are now busily engaged on upgrading or replacing the less satisfactory models in the range. DJH, after a somewhat chequered history, are pushing back the frontiers of the whitemetal kit with models that combine traditional cast components with photo-etched overlays and lost-wax details. The whitemetal locomotive kit has a lot of life left in it yet!

My own involvement with the whitemetal locomotive kit stretches back over twenty years, to the mid-1960s when, as a spotty schoolboy, I used to stick 'Finecast' kits together at the old Central Hall shows for Bob Wills. I suppose that he thought that the public, upon seeing Rice apparently getting somewhere with a whitemetal engine and a tube of Araldite, would be inspired to do likewise!

Since those heady days at Central Hall (whatever happened to all those part-built Woolwich Moguls, pannier tanks and Gresley Pacifics, I wonder?) I have got through well on the high side of three hundred whitemetal engines. For some several years, I struggled to earn a crust by building such models, which is no way to get rich as any bank manager will tell you! Gradually, I evolved and refined my own approach to these models, which is what I have expounded in these pages, and taught for some years at the summer courses we run here in Devon.

This book is an attempt to cram between two card covers as much of what I have learned as possible. I make no claims to being any great shakes as a loco builder — indeed, I would cite that as my principal qualification for writing about the subject. What I manage to achieve is well within the common province. I also build my models to run on my own, and other people's, layouts, rather than to grace showcases and win competitions.

I still enjoy building a good whitemetal kit, and I still think that, in most ways, whitemetal kits are the most practical way to assemble a representative stud of well-detailed, realistic model locomotives for a working layout. Over three-quarters of the motive power on my own layout started out thus. And I am still busy for Finecast, working on the upgrading of some of those kits that I used to stick together at Westminster twenty-odd years ago.

Mind you, this is not to imply that the whitemetal kit has reached some state of perfection. Far from it, and I have some pretty stringent criticisms to make about much that is found within those alluring cardboard boxes on the dealer's shelves. I don't suppose the words of Rice will be too well received in some quarters! But that is of no account, and if perhaps a little gentle pressure in the right places can bring about the elimination of some of the less satisfactory aspects of the whitemetal locomotive, then I shall have handed out my brickbats to some effect.

This has not been an easy topic to cover in a book, and I daresay that there is herein much that is not strictly relevant, and that which might be thought relevant will quite likely be found to be missing. It is a personal set of solutions, and has no claim to be absolute. Plenty of other people do it better, by different means. But, as I am often reminded, the wise man always keeps in mind that after the last word on anything there is always a full stop!

Iain Rice
Chagford
Devon

CHAPTER TWO

PRELIMINARIES, PHILOSOPHICAL AND PRACTICAL

A Nu-cast kit was the basis of Chris Pendlenton's V1 although extensive footplate modifications and new boiler fittings were needed for an accurate portrayal of this Tyneside stalwart.   CHRIS PENDLENTON

There is always a great temptation to set about the construction of a new locomotive with rather more vigour than forethought, by which I don't merely mean omitting the dry run usually advocated in the instructions, but also failing to think the whole model through to the desired conclusion. Are you working in EM? It is better to find out that the splashers need moving or the footplate cutting while the parts are still separate, accessible and easily worked. Does the kit suit the actual prototype loco you wish to model, or are there differences that might involve modifications, relocation of detail, extra parts?

And then there is the matter of standards, of the actual quality of the kit. The manufacturer is usually forced into a number of compromises, either by the material, the mould-making process or an unwillingness to get involved in complications such as the provision of certain parts in, say, etched brass, or lost-wax cast brass. Frequently, kits are tooled from inadequate or inaccurate drawings, which may also have been wrongly interpreted. Or the whole model may have been compromised to suit an unsuitable mechanism, or to use existing (but incorrect) patterns made for some other model. Wrong tenders are a frequent case in point.

And finally, there is the whole knotty area of the mechanical design of the kit. I must come into the open here, and state that I have consistently found the chassis design of so many of the whitemetal loco kits I've built vary from the poor to the absolutely appalling. It seems that all the good chassis-designers work for the etched-kit firms! So often I find that the chassis is crude, inaccurately made, gives no choice of motor/gearing arrangements to suit differing applications and looks nothing whatever like the prototype undercarriage. And I cannot for the life of me see the point of spending infinite time and trouble producing neat, accurate, well-detailed and carefully-painted superstructures — then sitting them on two slabs of wonky stamped brass, held loosely to spacers with very visible screws with heads a scale foot or two in diameter, finished off with a highly visible motor whirring busily where the firebox should be, not to mention erratic pick-ups trailing hither and thither, cabs full of magnet, big brass gears visible under the boiler, and a total lack of such fundamental chassis addenda as ashpans, sanding gear and brakes. The chassis is as much a part of the model as the chimney, the cab or the tender, and should receive the same care and consideration.

Furthermore, these criticisms take no account of the usual lack of any engineering thought in the design of the mechanism. Motor mountings, gear meshing, pick-ups and so on are more or less left to chance, glued in place maybe, or dependent upon one overlong screw in a hole several sizes too big. As a recipe for producing a sweet-running, reliable and robust mechanism, too many kit chassis are little better than throwing all the bits in a concrete-mixer and hoping for the best! Fortunately, there are now soundly-engineered alternatives available, while home-brewing a chassis is by no means as difficult as is often supposed. On the whole, you'd have a job to do worse than some of the kit-makers!

THE RIGHT APPROACH

What all this preamble boils down to is an attitude of mind, an approach to building the model that holds the end above the means. Instead of thinking: "I'm building a Finecast 'Hall' kit," the suggested stance runs rather more along the lines of "I'm building a model of GWR unmodified 'Hall' No. 6927 *Lilford Hall*, as running about 1935, using a Finecast kit.' The difference may be subtle, but it's significant. The kit is regarded with an eye positively yellow with jaundice, for it is mere clay, the stuff with which the work will be wrought.

To pursue this example a step or two further, what might the transformation of Finecast's lumps of alloy into *Lilford Hall* entail? Well, for a start, we find that Finecast supply the later Collett 4000-gallon riveted tender, and for our choice of prototype we need the original 3500-gallon flush-sided Churchward variety. Some correspondence with the maker to effect the swap is a first step. And then, the 'Hall' is one of those kits corrupted to take an R-T-R chassis that approximated to the prototype wheel size and spacing — a relic of the days when whitemetal kits were regarded merely as the means of extending a ready-to-run loco stud, rather than as the basis for accurate models of high quality. So remedial work will be needed in the matter of moving the rear splashers and the cylinders.

And what of that thick cast cab roof? Would not a thin brass one be a great improvement?

How about a lost-wax chimney with a nice copper rim, a proper brass safety valve bonnet, some turned smokebox darts? The loco-tender coupling will need closing up, and a set of turned sprung buffers will set off the front end. . . .

And then there is the chassis. The suggested Triang B12 unit is no longer available, and even if it were, the coarse steamroller wheels are too big and too close together and the motor sticks out in all sorts of undesired places. What then, of the alternatives? Wills offer a cast block to which you can at least fit the right size of wheel, but the wheelbase is still wrong (to suit the footplate which has the splashers cast in the wrong place to accommodate the aforementioned B12 chassis), and the motor is horribly visible where the firebox should be. All is not lost, however, for Perseverance in this case do an etched chassis kit which will suit just fine. Correct wheelbase, compensated, a lot easier to build than the kit effort, nice etched rods, brake gear, correct frame profile with cut-outs, rivet detail, a compensated bogie . . . All we have to do is move the errant splasher and we have the basis of a good model.

The Perseverance chassis also gives us freedom of choice in the matter of gauge (00, EM, or P4 all catered for), motor type, motor mounting, gear ratio, pick-up type and location, and, of course, wheel make, type and standard. It is, in other words, the sort of chassis that should be supplied with the loco kit in the first place!

All this, of course, is well and good, but displays the usual callous disregard for money that so distresses my bank manager! By the time we have purchased our kit, chucked away umpteen bits as not being up to scratch, bought additional parts, swapped tenders, and then provided ourselves with a Perseverance chassis kit, a motor, gearset and a sufficiency of wheels, our 'Hall' is starting to look like an expensive proposition. This may be so, but then, we have the potential for a high-class model which, ipso facto, will be worth more at the end of the day. We also have control over vital mechanical choices, and are not forced to accept unwanted compromises which sap the satisfaction from the modelling process. And is it so expensive? Staying with our example, we note that the basic Wills Kit contains loco body and tender complete. The chassis was an addition anyway. The tender exchange is a trifle of postage, only the 'extras' need providing. The level of refinement is a function of individual resources and commitment; the copper-top chimney is a nicety, not a necessity. The motor could be a second-hand XO4, or a brand-new RG4. And there is no reason why you should not fret out your own frames, file up coupling-rods, fabricate brake gear.

As is so often the case in the model railway hobby, we have a triangular equation of time against money against satisfaction. How you

Sub-assemblies are an excellent idea, both for building and painting. The 'H' class has a less usual divide, with the boiler and tank tops separating from the rest of the loco.

The J39 sub-assemblies. In this instance the backhead is mounted directly on the boiler, which locates through the cabfront in prototypical fashion.

strike the balance is up to you, but I suspect that a majority are short of time, and thus up the money to buy in bits to save that irreplaceable commodity, at the additional expense of a little satisfaction. If satisfaction is all, cut the money right down and build your loco from scratch from salvaged tin cans! At the end of the day, I know I'd rather have a few locos that I knew were as good as I could make 'em, rather than two dozen compromised, inaccurate bodge-ups.

Having disposed of the philosophy, it is now time to turn the spotlight on practical matters and get to grips with our kit. The next step might be considered more theoretical than practical, but it is practically a necessity: planning. The instructions will hopefully give some clues as to how the model is intended to go together, though so often they are a compound of bad grammar, bad drawings, close-typed mumbo-jumbo lacking punctuation, and wishful thinking.

Planning has two aspects. Firstly, we need some prototype reference material for our

chosen engine, so that we may determine what alterations and additions are going to be needed to make the model conform. A drawing is not essential, but photographs are, the more the better, hopefully showing several aspects of the subject. This is not always easy, particularly when it comes to the less photogenic aspects of locomotive anatomy. Books are one source, prototype literature (*Railway Magazine*, etc.), specialist publications such as the *British Railway Journal*, *HMRS Journal* or the various profile/portrait studies another. Best of all are the photo lists from firms such as Photomatic, Real Photos, HMRS, and so on. It is often possible to acquire several views of a particular engine through these various sources. The bibliography at the end of this book gives more details of where prototype information might be sought.

Where information is not forthcoming, we may have to resort to deduction or inspired guesswork. The kit will hopefully have some basis of research, so our errors should only be matters of detail. How much this worries you is again a matter of individual standards. For myself, I tend to settle for the amount of data I can assemble reasonably easily from obvious sources. If some smart Alec comes along later with carping criticism, I usually pick his brains for further information, before inviting him to up soldering-iron and make a better job of it . . . Usually, the error will be trivial enough to either change without major disturbance of the model, or be small enough to ignore. In instances where a real booboo has been unwittingly perpetrated, I'm afraid I opt for the easy option — find a prototype that conforms to the model, and change the number. . . .

The second planning aspect concerns the purely practical. If surgery is needed (as for that errant splasher on the 'Hall') then it will need doing at the right stage. A change of chassis design or motor type or location may need allowing for, and any extra clearances must be provided or redundant holes or openings stopped up. Then, there is the matter of painting, which merits consideration at this early stage. Will the loco be easier to paint if it breaks down into sub-assemblies? A classic case is the lined cab front, a whole lot easier to execute if the boiler is a separate unit that can be got out of the way whilst the tricky stuff with the bow-pen is taking place. This may also make it easier to apply the boiler

bands, and help ensure that the bottom of the boiler gets properly painted.

Practical planning is often a case of 'suck-it-and-see'. Will an RG4 motor go in? Mock up the relevant castings with Blu-tak and try it. Don't want to buy an RG4 just to find it won't fit? A Plastikard mock-up at full size takes only minutes to build, and is a useful planning tool. So long as the basic dimensions are accurate, it can be rough as old boots. If the RG4 won't go, try a Plastikard D13 or what have you till you find a set-up that works. Using this technique, and ignoring the kit recommendation (usually based on the assumption that the only motor existing in the world is an XO4 or one of its clones) it is often possible to regain daylight under the boiler or free cabs of large chunks of magnetised iron, simply by experi-

menting with different motor types, locations and driven axles.

Having waded through all these preliminaries, it is at long last time to actually get to grips with the kit. I intend at this juncture to utterly ignore the chassis (although in point of fact I usually build it first), and get straight on with the assembly of the cast locomotive body.

TOOLS

Few are the tools needed to assemble a cast locomotive body. For preparing the castings, I find the most valuable implement to be a 3-sided scraper, obtainable from good tool-smiths like Shestophal. In addition, I acquire a selection of emery boards as purveyed by Boots for the shaping of the female talon, plus

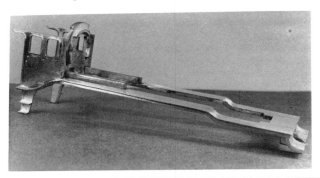

Here is a major sub-assembly of the K3 basically complete.

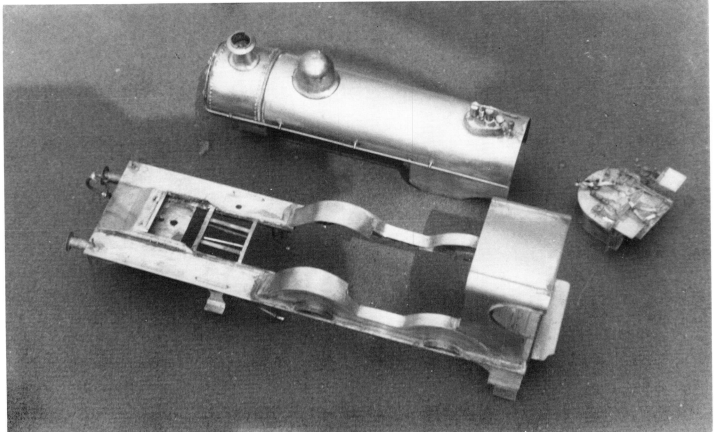

Here is a typical 'breakdown' for a 4—4—0, scratchbuilt in this instance, but a cast one would divide in the same way. Footplate with cab, boiler, and cab interior.

A corner of the work-shop, with loco kits under construction during a model railway study centre course. The workboard, soldering station and Anglepoise lamp are the basic essentials.

a few knackered files and a fibre-glass burnishing stick. It is no use buying good files for this work, you'll only ruin them and anyway they are little used. I find a great big bastard cut flat mill file good for getting rid of major amounts of whitemetal, and French chalk or talc will help keep it clean. Otherwise I do all my cleaning up with the scraper and emery boards. I also make rubbing sticks of various odd sizes and shapes by sticking wet-and-dry paper (240 and 400 grit) to bits of wood, usually ¼″ square spruce obtained from the local model aircraft emporium. A scalpel and a Stanley knife can be useful, while for cutting the whitemetal in operations such as opening out footplate clearances for EM, I use bits of broken coarse hack-saw blade, or wood fretsaw blades in the piercing saw.

To actually assemble the castings, I use an 18W SRB soldering iron, phosphoric acid flux and low-melt (70°) alloy. Other 'tools' include clothes pegs, bulldog clips, Dinky hair curlers, a few small blocks of wood, Plasticine and Blu-tak, a good pair of tweezers and a set of asbestos fingers. Glues various do not agree with me, but there are those who like them, and they can at least dispense with the asbestos fingers!

Other tools needed are a small sharpened screwdriver, for getting solder out of right-angled seams and other tidying-up operations, a pin-vice and a few small drills, plus a taper brooch or two. A few Plastikard offcuts are useful for mixing/applying filler if needed, though I do most of my filling with solder as I assemble. Where I need a chemical filler, I find Isopon and cellulose body putty serve well, but there are umpteen alternatives.

Other requirements for whitemetal loco building are few. A work-place is needed, preferably well lit. A vice is handy but not essential, and I also like to provide myself with a few lidded containers to keep all the tiddly bits from getting lost. In practice, a good deal of the job, especially preparation, can be comfortably and sociably accomplished on an old tea tray on the knee, whilst occupying a favourite chair in front of the fire.

We have now selected our kit, purchased it, acquired all the necessary bits and pieces, indulged in correspondence with the manufacturer, undertaken a trifle of research, and spent a little time in thought. From now on, things get physical.

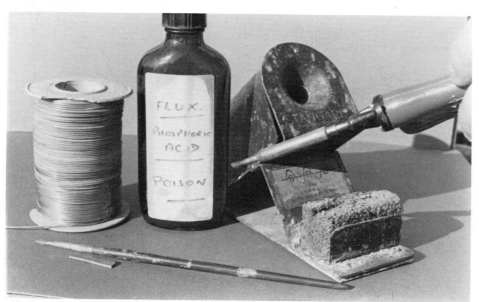

Soldering necessities — iron with stand and cleaning sponge, phosphoric flux, flux brush, 145° wire solder and 70° cast-kit solder.

CHAPTER THREE

PREPARING THE CASTINGS

At last it is time to tip out the contents of the box, with which we are by now thoroughly familiar, and get to work turning all these meaningless chunks of cast alloy into a locomotive. Before starting on the real business of assembly, however, we must prepare the castings.

Good castings will need little preparation, so hopefully a few passes with the scraper to part off the wafer-thin flash that even the best moulds are apt to leave should be all that is required. Oh that all castings were good castings! It is an imperfect world that we live in, and the chances are that some if not all of our castings will need a great deal more preparation than this!

Once again, it is important to bear in mind the object of the exercise: to remove all imperfections while retaining the details that the patternmaker has laboured long and hard to incorporate. We do not want a blitzkrieg of the surface, reducing once-clean and crisp beading and rivets to indeterminate, faint rounded bumps and ridges. Which means goodbye to brass suede brushes and other instruments of violence often recommended by the more macho school of kit construction. Sure, they produce a nice shiny silver model — minus most of the detail, scratched to blazes and a lousy basis for the paint!

Far better to work with the model, not against it. Consider each casting carefully, and remove flash or feed-nibs carefully, maybe in several small bits rather than one hefty cut. The whitemetal is intrinsically soft, and sharp tools have a nasty tendency to dig in, with unfortunate results. This is the advantage conferred by the three-sided scraper, with its 60° cutting edge and flat reference faces; the cutting edge passes over the surface of the metal, levelling the imperfections without tending to produce hollows or chew unwanted bites from the hapless casting. It pays to keep at least one edge of the scraper good and sharp — a small stone on the bench to 'touch-up' this 'prime' edge is no bad idea. I also keep one edge fairly dull, where mere gentle abrasion is enough to remove thin casting flash.

There are some components that are best cleaned up after at least some initial assembly. Boiler halves are a case in point. There will be flash and several mould part lines to deal with, and I find it usually pays to solder up the boiler, fill the top seam, and then set to work to both remove unwanted metal and to make the boiler as near round as possible. Working on curved components such as a boiler barrel provides more problems if we are not to end up 'three-penny bitting' (or should it be '50p piecing'?) the boiler. It is imperative to keep the tool, whatever it might be, working around the curve of the boiler at around 45° to the axis of the barrel. A tool used along the boiler or directly across it almost inevitably results in 'flats'.

WORKING ON CURVED SURFACES

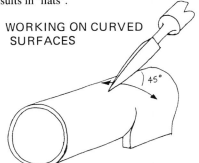

This, of course, presents a major problem. Boilers tend to have boiler bands, which are at right-angles to the axis and thus get plumb in the way of cleaning-up operations conducted at the recommended 45°. If you are intent upon preserving such bands, then I'm afraid compromise is necessary, and very delicate work with file, scraper and emery board parallel to the bands is the only answer. Go very gingerly, only taking light cuts, and check frequently to make sure the tool is not cutting a nasty flat. I find that the emery board is most useful in this situation, as it abrades rather than cuts the surface.

However, I usually employ a far more drastic remedy to the boiler band problem; I lop

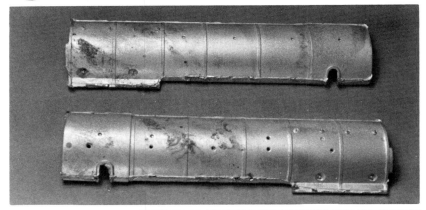

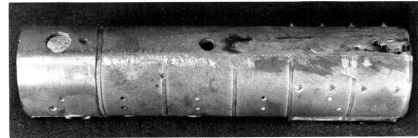

Boilers are best prepared 'in the round'. Here, the two halves of the K3 boiler casting have been soldered together, and the top seam filled with lowmelt. The complete boiler is then dressed down with a coarse file, followed by scrapers and finishing with wet-and-dry on a rubbing block. The boiler bands are removed at the same time.

'em off. This may seem to contradict the advocated 'gently, gently, sparee detail' approach, but I regard boiler bands as one of the less successful elements of cast loco kits. Due to the shrinkage properties, they almost never line up across the boiler-top joint, which makes it very difficult to dress them into a convincing semblance of continuity. Also, they are usually

a smooth, even surface. We are doing the same, in miniature.

Mould flash has a nasty habit of cutting right across detail at some point or other, when one is faced with the inevitable impasse of removing both flash and detail, or neither. Again, the boiler usually provides a good headache of this type, in the form of smokebox wrappers bespattered with a row or two of rivets. These

are inexorably entwined with anything up to four mould part lines plus the joint seam where the boiler halves meet.

As I have yet to see a prototype locomotive with a mould part line halfway up the smokebox, I give priority to the removal of this unwanted piece of topography, at the expense of the detail. Once I have removed the imperfection, I take a look at the damage to the detail, to see whether I can live with it. Where only one or two rivets are involved, I might let it go. Three to six, I'll probably reinstate individually, using the wire-in-a-hole method which is fully described in the chapter on basic

Alan Ketley's superb award-winning 'Merchant Navy'. A perfect illustration of just what is possible with a whitemetal kit.

grossly over-scale, and often need lining as well. As the accepted method of lining boiler bands is to paint and line a strip of adhesive tape or paper, and stick this in place on the painted model, what purpose does the cast band serve? Merely to make the final, painted job look over-prominent — a prototype boiler band being only around 1/8″ thick. So I dispense with these troublesome protuberances at the cleaning up stage, and reinstate them as part of the painting process. The scraper is again the implement to use, sharp edge foremost, and working at the 45° angle that is now no problem!

When removing unwanted detail such as the hapless boiler bands, I do the bulk of the cutting with the scraper, and finish off with an emery board or rubbing stick. What I never do is to use an unsupported piece of wet-and-dry paper, wrapped around a finger end or rolled up. This inevitably results in a hollow, whereas abrasive paper properly supported, as on an emery board or rubbing stick, will only cut that metal which is proud of the general surface. Watch a good carpenter or car-body repair man rubbing-down to see how they rely on a flat backing to their abrasives to achieve

USING ABRASIVE PAPERS

ABRASIVE PAPER

X UNSUPPORTED - TENDS TO WEAR A HOLLOW.

WOOD BLOCK

✓ SUPPORTED - GIVES A FLAT SURFACE.

detailing. Where a good proportion of the rivets have been sacrificed, then more drastic remedies are called for. The rest of the rivets may be taken off, and that particular refinement ignored. Or, more likely, I'll set to and produce a smokebox wrapper from thin brass, Plastikard, or even paper, in which case, I can emboss the rivet detail on the wrapper.

By the by, it is always worth consulting your prototype photos to check that the particular loco you are modelling does have snap-headed rivets at that location. Nothing is more aggravating than to spend time and trouble reinstating rivets that you later find the real engine didn't have! I know, I've done it. Smokeboxes are again a particular case in point; often some members of a given class had flush riveted smokeboxes — no visible rivet heads — while others had snap rivets. Or the same engine might have an original flush-riveted smokebox

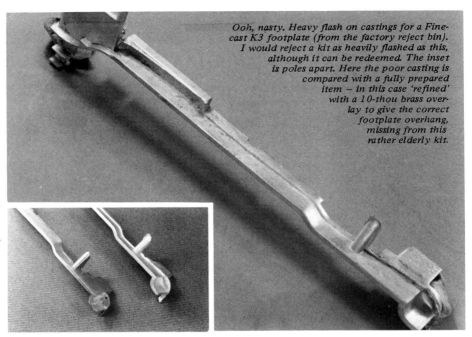

Ooh, nasty. Heavy flash on castings for a Fine-cast K3 footplate (from the factory reject bin). I would reject a kit as heavily flashed as this, although it can be redeemed. The inset is poles apart. Here the poor casting is compared with a fully prepared item — in this case 'refined' with a 10-thou brass overlay to give the correct footplate overhang, missing from this rather elderly kit.

replaced by snap-heads during re-boilering, at general overhaul or on repair after damage.

Where the mould registration has not been well-controlled during manufacture, mould part lines can manifest themselves as considerable 'steps' in the surface, requiring treatment more drastic than a few passes of the scraper. If you are as choosy as I am about kit purchase, the problem won't arise, as you won't have bought such a ropy specimen in the first place!

Here is the other end of the same K3 castings, showing the result of a little 'fining-down' of the cabsides and rear steps.

If it is really bad, it might be well to consider sending the offending casting back for replacement, which, if nothing else, makes the manufacturer aware of the problem.

However, often matters are not that bad, but still require some rectification, which is where we get a bit more heavy-handed and really start chivvying the metal about. The problem is usually at its worst, once again, on boiler and smokebox, which is where I wheel out my biggest gun, the mill bastard file. As I'm never too concerned about keeping the boiler bands, it is usually only smokebox rivets and maybe the odd firebox washout plug or mud door that will really suffer. So be it. The top of the boiler on a model loco is very visible, and must present a smooth unbroken contour not a series

of steps, ridges and flats. Washout plugs and rivets can be reinstated, so I grit my teeth, seize Big Bertha, set up the boiler in the vice, on a V-block or in a big lump of Plasticine, and set to.

Once again, it is essential to cut at 45° to the axis, working the file round the curve of the boiler. Talc on the job helps keep the white-metal from blocking the file, which anyway has less tendency to clog up as it is scarcely a fine cut! As soon as I've got rid of the worst of the 'step', I retire Big Bertha in favour of a smaller file, then the scraper, the emery boards and finally a rubbing stick covered in 400 grit wet-and-dry. Keep squinting at the shape you are producing, preferably in a good directional light, to make sure you are getting as close an approximation as possible to a truly cylindrical shape.

Obviously, one undertakes this rather drastic process with as much regard for the detail in the castings as is practicable, but once again it is a case of setting the end above the means. A wonky, misshapen boiler with a full complement of rivets looks far worse than a smooth, round one with the odd snap-head absent. And it is often better in the long run to add certain details separately that kit-makers tend to try and cast-on, boiler pipework such as blower feeds or vacuum ejectors being cases in point.

In any case, some of the detail that is often incorporated in castings may be unconvincing, and better replaced by other components added to the model. Pipework is a common example, there being no doubt that wire or rod of appropriate diameter looks a lot better than a half-round bump on the casting. So, whilst I have my scraper to hand, I take a good look at such features with my most sceptical eye. There is no doubt that this is one area where applying the 'building-a-model-using-a-kit' rather than the 'building-a-kit' approach can result in a final job that is individual, more convincing and thus, ultimately, more satisfying. It's an aspect of the process that I call 'refining' a kit, taking out those compromises that the manufacturer, through expediency, necessity or with an eye to his (very necessary) profit margin has accepted.

There is no doubt that the poor old kit manufacturer is caught in a cleft stick over this one. The market expects a kit these days to be both complete and well-detailed. The whitemetal kit-maker is committed to his material, which does not necessarily lend itself to the production of all the necessary bits for a given locomotive. Hence all those wonky, over-fragile and impossible-to-clean-up detail castings — ejector pipes, vacuum hoses, whistles, smoke-box darts and so on — which are far better represented in materials other than whitemetal. (Many etched kits are equally guilty of this sort of thing, with 'cardboard cut-out' springs, outside cranks and so on; OK in profile, but miles too thin.) The answer comes back, as usual, to cost and ease of manufacture. If the

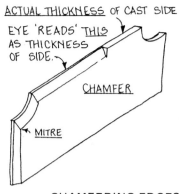

**CHAMFERING EDGES
FOR THAT 'THIN' LOOK**

kit-maker has to buy-in and keep in stock all manner of bits and pieces, sizes of wire and rod, small etchings and so on, it makes his life more difficult and the supply of the kits on which his livelihood depends more erratic. Hence the temptation to 'cast and be damned', even if some of the resulting components are a bit impracticable.

A lot of small components, be they cast, etched or whatever, also make packing more difficult and time-consuming, and the chances of error much higher. Hence the additional temptation to cast as much of the detail as possible integral with the main components. Speaking personally, I would rather pay a pound or two more for my kit and have the detail represented by the best possible material, and I'm glad to see one or two of the more enterprising whitemetal kit-makers moving away from the 'cast-and-be-damned' philosophy of yore. Some, such as DJH, have gone as far as to produce major 'sheet' components as etchings, to be attached to the otherwise cast components. As we shall show, soldering a sheet-brass cabside or roof to a cast cab-front is not at all difficult, and can significantly upgrade the model.

So, as part of the preparation process, I am also looking closely at the castings to see which detail I am happy with, and which detail or components I reckon I can improve upon. Often, I do the looking at the planning stage, but, even so, I often notice things when I'm preparing the castings that suggest themselves as candidates for improvement.

Such improvement does not always involve removal of cast detail or the scrapping of cast parts in favour of other materials or components. Often, it can merely involve the modification of the casting in quite subtle ways — the 'refining' process to which I have already referred. The most obvious improvement that can be made to castings representing sheet components — cab and tender sides, roofs, footplate edges and so on — is to taper the

edge of the inevitably over-thick casting so that it presents a thin line to the viewer. This is simply accomplished with the scraper, file and emery boards, and can do much to take away the 'chunky' look that so often spoils a model built from a cast kit. After all, which real locomotive do you know of with cab and tender sides a full 3 inches thick?

The 'refining' process can also be advantageously applied to detail such as beading, frequently over-thick and heavy (to make sure it casts properly and comes out of the mould without breaking away), cab rainstrips, spectacle rims, footsteps, and sometimes rivet or bolt-heads. Gentle, careful work with the scraper, a small square file and rubbing sticks can 'fine-down' such features, with benefit to the fidelity of the model.

A word at this point about the degree of 'finish' we are aiming for on the castings. I have stressed (I hope) the necessity to proceed with caution and delicacy. Whitemetal is a material of fine crystalline structure that takes fine impressions and is easily damaged or marked. A light touch and consideration of the necessity to avoid tools 'digging-in' is paramount, and the moderate and reasoned use of abrasives should result in a surface that is smooth, clean, bright but certainly not polished. A light burnishing with a fibreglass stick is the most that I ever permit myself in this direction, and I read with horror the advice sometimes given for polishing the metal with abrasives, brass brushes and even Brasso! This is death to the crispness of the model, dulling and rounding all the edges, blurring detail and leaving all manner of residues in the surface layer of the metal to impede soldering and painting. What we are aiming at is a model locomotive, not some emulation of a chrome-laden 1950s Cadillac.

There is one other aspect of surface finish which we may look at in the preparation stage, and that is the elimination of that old enemy of the fine finish (and another classic white-metal 'giveaway'), the porous boiler, tender or cabside already mentioned. A little porosity is often inevitable on some of the heftier castings such as boiler halves or cabsides. If really bad, we will hopefully have avoided it by not buying the kit in the first place. We may just have the odd porous casting, and it may be worth considering returning this to the manufacturer for replacement. This is particularly valid where the casting so afflicted carries a lot of surface detail — riveted tender sides are frequent culprits. It is difficult to take effective remedial action without damaging or obscuring the detail.

Where the pock-marks afflict only some nice unencumbered surface such as the boiler (probably already devoid of boiler bands for the reasons noted), then it is possible to effect a very complete and undetectable remedy by dosing the area concerned thoroughly with phosphoric acid flux, and flooding a layer of

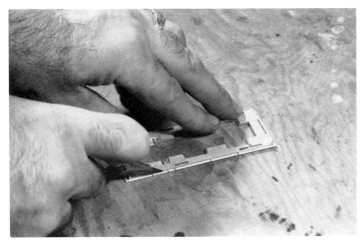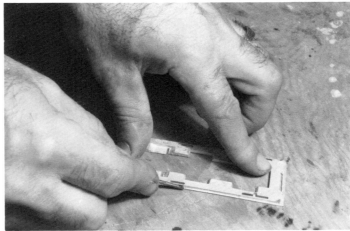

This is a J69 footplate casting straight out of the box, showing the feed 'nibs' along the valance. The sequence shows these being removed, using the sharpened screwdriver and scraper.

low-melt alloy onto the surface. The flux will boil away, creating tiny vacuums in the open pores of the porous metal which draw in the molten alloy to form a complete seal. The surface can then be dressed with scraper and abrasives in the normal way. I treat porous metal in this way before undertaking general cleaning-up and preparation of the casting concerned, when the excess metal can be treated as just one more casting blemish.

Where this highly satisfactory approach cannot be adopted (it is intrinsically the same as 'leading' a car body to eliminate corrosion pits or scratches in steel), then we must resort to chemical fillers or varnishes, which is really part of the finishing and painting process, and will be described at that point in this narrative.

The last preparatory job we must undertake is that of fitting. Only a certain amount of this can be done before assembly commences, but it is certainly well worth having a 'dry-run' and correcting the more obvious anomalies. We have already noted the liability of white-metal castings to a certain dimensional instability during manufacture, and while our critical selection of the kit should ensure that the major components are within a few percent of their true size, a bit of dressing with a file will doubtless be needed. The usual culprits are the boiler halves (again!), footplates, particularly those cast in several pieces, and tender sides. The worst case I ever encountered was a large tank locomotive by one of the lesser lights of the cast-kit world, where an attempt had been made to cast the entire loco in two halves (footplate/sidetanks/cab/bunker sides). These two massive castings varied in length by nearly 3/16″! An error so gross as to defy any remedial attempt on my part.

The N7 bunkerside and tanks had some rather obtrusive 'dimples' from the ends of dowels holding the patterns together. These can be seen to the left of the cab door, whilst those on the bunkerside were filled with lowmelt, then dressed down.

The usual 1 mm or so that might be typically exhibited can be accommodated by a modicum of filing, fitting and a trifle of filling during assembly. To undertake and assess this necessary work, I test-assemble the loco 'dry' on a true surface such as plateglass, holding it all together with Blu-tak. It is then a matter of checking for alignment, using a small square, a straight edge and the usual jaundiced eye. One check that is very important to undertake is the footplate alignment. This often involves the longest castings in the kit, and as well as shrinkage it is often found that the castings are bowed or warped, requiring a little careful remedial bending. Fingers not pliers, please! I also check that the footplate edges are parallel, and find it is not unusual to have a footplate tapering in plan by a millimetre or so. A bit of dressing on the widest footplate spacer is the usual remedy, accomplished by rubbing the offending casting gently on my big file laid flat on the bench.

This is a general technique used to ensure a true edge; if you file the component by gripping it and applying the file to the edge, the result is almost inevitably a gentle parabolic curve, which is not too helpful if the component you're filing is going to determine how 'square' the model goes together. It's much the same problem as rubbing at a casting with unsupported abrasive paper; without a reference surface, an irregular result is more than likely. By laying the file flat on the bench, the file itself is the reference, and by gently sliding the casting to and fro, there's a much better chance of ending up with a true edge.

There is obviously a limit as to how far the fitting process can be taken at the 'dry run' stage; I tend to restrict myself to the major components, undertaking all other sizing work in the course of assembly. However, I have found that the less impediment there is to the actual business of soldering the components of the kit together, the smoother, more fluid and ultimately more successful the whole business becomes.

You will have inferred from the foregoing that I consider the preparation and refinement of the castings to be the very foundation of a successful kit-built locomotive. Indeed, I usually spend a lot longer preparing the kit than I do assembling it (although detailing and finishing takes longer still). Building a good model locomotive from a whitemetal kit is quicker than building from scratch; but it's not that much quicker if the result is to be in any way comparable. The 'five-minute wonder' school of kit assembly rarely realise anything approaching the full potential of the kit.

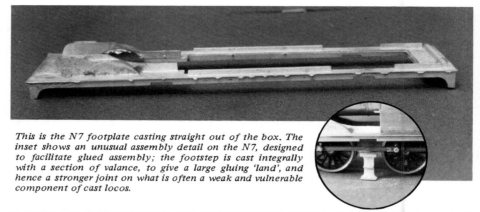

This is the N7 footplate casting straight out of the box. The inset shows an unusual assembly detail on the N7, designed to facilitate glued assembly; the footstep is cast integrally with a section of valance, to give a large gluing 'land', and hence a stronger joint on what is often a weak and vulnerable component of cast locos.

The N7 footplate also had a nasty nick out of the footplate angle at the rear end. This was made good by blobbing on some solder and filing to shape.

CHAPTER FOUR
ASSEMBLY TECHNIQUES

The actual sequence of assembly of a white-metal kit is really impossible to discuss in the context of a book, as it will vary so radically from kit to kit. By and large, the kit instructions will indicate the most suitable order in which the parts are fitted and joined, although considerations of detailing or painting may suggest some deviations. I have already noted my preference for sub-assemblies, and for the actual assembly of certain items before cleaning-up. I suppose that the only generality that may be usefully observed is that, as a rule, the foundation of most model locomotive superstructures is the footplate, so this may commonly be the best place to start; it is probably the most critical assembly in terms of the quality of the finished job.

Otherwise, assembly consists of the actual physical joining of the various castings to form an homogeneous whole. This process comprises two stages — fitting and securing. Most of the former is, I have suggested, done as part of the pre-assembly preparation, leaving only the odd bit of fettling to be tackled as part of the actual assembly work. Apart from all else, I like to keep the bench as clear and as clean as possible, and obviously the fewer processes in hand, the easier this is to accomplish.

As the fitting techniques used during assembly vary not one whit from those used prior to assembly, I shall say no more about them here. What I am much more concerned about is the means by which the castings are united:

> To glue, or not to glue, that is the question,
> Whether 'tis nobler in the kit to offer the
> cyanos and epoxies of outrageous stiction,
> Or to take irons amid a sea of solder, And
> by a-heating fix them?

ADHESIVES

I suppose that the word 'gluing' may merit a little qualification. In days of yore, when K's still lurked in the nether regions of West London, they used to recommend a glue called Pafra — long vanished. This was great stuff, a sort of Neanderthal Bostik — except that it went brittle after a while, and tended to lose cohesion. Then, one day, you were perchance a trifle unhandy coming into your terminus and smote the stopblocks a bit hard — whereupon your locomotive resolved itself into its component parts in spectacular fashion! The results were roughly on a par with a boiler explosion, so far as the locomotive was concerned. No great recommendation for gluing as a sound method of kit assembly!

Nowadays, we are far better placed for adhesives, and my own experience tends towards conventional two-part epoxy resin. In the days

when I used to demonstrate kit assembly on the Wills stand at Central Hall, I used to have about 15 locos on the go, all at some stage in the 24-hour curing cycle of the Araldite then available, which Bob Wills advocated. The vision of lots of melted bits winging in by every post would give him sleepless nights, so I was never allowed to demonstrate solder assembly!

To glue, or not to glue? . . . epoxy, cyanogel, epoxy filler, cellulose stopping.

These days, there are quick-cure epoxies which bond to reasonable strength in 5–10 minutes, and these are certainly a better bet, if a trifle wasteful in use — one never seems to use up more than a fraction of each 'mix' before it goes off. The great advantage of epoxy resins over other adhesives such as cyano-acrylates is that they cure chemically by catalytic action, and are of a consistency that permits of their limited use as a filler. The 'super-glues', so called, act in the exclusion of air, and are only really effective in very close-fitting joints — far from typical in most whitemetal kits!

Some people take the 'glue-as-filler' approach a stage further and use a filler as glue. Two materials that offer possibilities in this direction are Plastic Padding type Elastic, and Milliput. The first is basically a two-part resin with metallic powder filler, but which has pretty good adhesion characteristics. The second material is an epoxy putty, again a form of filled resin, and though rather laborious in use — the two components of the putty must be thoroughly kneaded together like some demonic dough — is very strong, easily worked and of good surface when set. Milliput is particularly useful for repairing damaged castings, filling in unwanted holes and even adding details like superheater headers. I do have my reservations about the final strength

of a model held together only by the adhesive action of a filler — after all, adhesion is not the prime function of the material, and it is to a certain extent being misused.

There is no doubt that the success of a glued model depends very greatly on thorough preparation of the metal for the adhesive. No glue bonds well to a layer of grease, dirt and oxide, so scrupulous surface cleaning is *de rigueur*. De-greasing is a prime requirement, and really needs an effective solvent to remove all trace of sweat, skin grease from your hands, and oil trace from tools. I find non-lubricating switch-cleaner, sold in aerosol cans by better radio and electronic shops to be effective, if a trifle pricey. Meths also seems to work quite well, and one or two proprietary stain removers (Thawpit) will serve. Lighter fuel can also be used, but I can't say I care much for the fire and fume hazards from any of these. Work in a well-ventilated space, and don't smoke. Otherwise you may have a genuine boiler explosion on your hands!

Once you have prepared the joint faces for gluing by rubbing lightly with a coarse abrasive (to provide a key), and cleaning as described, the glue should be mixed and applied, and the joint made as fast as possible. The components will need support and location, preferably under slight pressure, while the adhesive cures. Blu-tak, Plasticine, clothes-pegs, blocks of wood, weights and rubber bands are all useful adjuncts to glued construction.

The other vital requirement is patience. Premature handling is the Achilles' heel of the glued joint, so it pays to have a sticking session last thing at night, to give it all a chance to cure while you're snatching the nightly repose deep in the arms of Morpheus. A little heat

A DJH BR Standard 2—6—4T, built for 18.83mm gauge by Alan Ketley. Meticulous attention to detail pays off.

will help things along — the airing cupboard, near to a night-storage heater, or the top of the central-heating boiler are good places.

The successful assembly of a kit by gluing is, to a considerable extent, dependent upon the 'fit' of the kit. Adhesives are, as a rule, designed to bond two surfaces in actual contact over the desired joining area. Unfortunately, there are all too many whitemetal locomotive kits where this desirable state of affairs is largely absent — hence the use of fillers as adhesives. As an alternative to this, the joint may be reinforced by gluing a bracing patch on the rear of the job. This will give much greater mechanical strength, and the filler will then be required only to fulfil the function for which it was formulated.

FILLING
All whitemetal kits need a certain amount of filling, and a good few need a lot of work to present a smooth, unbroken surface for the finish. I divide filling into two stages, 'primary filling' and 'finish filling'.

Primary filling, as its name implies, aims to eliminate major gaps and hollows, and is undertaken during assembly. If soldered construction is being employed, the primary filling and assembly is simultaneous, as the solder will, by the nature of its action, fill cracks and crannies as it flows between the castings being joined. Where the castings have been glued, then there will need to be an actual application of filler. Let the adhesive cure fully first, though — many a model have I seen riven asunder by the enthusiastic application of filler to joints that were still 'soft'! The filler itself wants to be semi-liquid and easily worked. For this reason, I prefer to use the type of filler that is sold with resin, catalyst and filler powder as separate components. That way I can control the consistency of The Vital Mix.

On the subject of that mix — small quantities is the rule. Otherwise the temptation to try and use filler that has started to 'go off' will be the more frequent. It should be resisted at all costs. Resin that has started to react will not flow, nor will it self-level, and its adhesion and surface are impaired. Do be careful, too, to get the resin/catalyst proportions accurate, otherwise you may get filler that will never cure properly, giving a nasty, sticky surface that will not file or sand, and which will do funny things when you try to paint it. The products I use in the primary filling role (where, for some reason, I can't use solder assembly) are David's 'Isopon' or Holts 'Cataloy', both of which are available in three-part from.

Finish filling is only intended to take care of minor blemishes and surface dressing of cracks, hollows and filled holes. It is really part of the painting and finishing process, and I will deal with it fully at that juncture.

UNGLUING
One last aspect of glued construction that can sometimes be a real problem—that of ungluing. Not in the sense of 'coming unglued' so much as in the terrible realisation that you have glued on part A too soon and now cannot fit part B. And the carefully-cured Araldite holding A in place shows no sign of wanting to facilitate the temporary removal of A in favour of B! The answer is Nitromors paintstripper (type Yellow) — nasty stuff needing care in handling, but vicious enough to soften Araldite so that it can be cut with a sharp knife. Soak the offending joint overnight in the smallest practicable quantity of the Nitromors. As an aside, a Nitromors bath does a fine job of reducing a poorly-assembled and badly painted whitemetal kit (such as might be purchased very cheaply secondhand) to its component parts, unpainted and ready for cleaning up and

re-assembly. In my impecunious student days I had quite a stud of locos built from kits 'rescued' in this fashion. You need enough Nitromors to completely cover the model, and it'll need to soak for days rather than hours. There is a certain satisfaction gained from turning a real horror-job of a model into something presentable, quite apart from the sound economics of the process.

SOLDER ASSEMBLY
From all of the foregoing it will be inferred — correctly — that I have found gluing infinitely more troublesome and less reliable than the solder-assembly of whitemetal kits. To someone of my mercurial temperament (all right, so I'm downright impatient!), a process that requires frequent, prolonged breaks to allow adhesives to achieve a good bond is fraught with dangers and frustrations. Solder, on the other hand, will have developed full strength before it's cool enough to handle with comfort. Unless you've got asbestos fingers, you will not have many problems with joints moving before they 'set'. Solder also allows infinite adjustment, and is, as previously remarked, largely self-filling. And the oft-cited danger of the kit melting away before your very eyes into a Dali-esque 'soft loco' is much exaggerated, and largely due to misunderstanding of the process and materials.

SOLDERS
We are apt, in this hobby, to use terminology somewhat loosely. Thus, we talk glibly of 'low-melt solder', without really defining (or thinking of) what we really mean. What, for instance, is 'normal-melt solder'? And how low is low? I have taken, in recent years, to defining the actual melting point when I'm discussing solders, as this is the only way we can really be certain that we are understanding

the same thing when we talk of 'low melt'. I suppose the normal conception of 'normal melt' would be the traditional tinman's solder, although even this comes in different grades with different melting points. However, the 50/50 Multicore (green and red pack; roughly 50% tin, 50% lead) that has been 'staple fare' for a number of years melts at around 375°C. The newer generation of electronic solders (GPO grade, Brewster's Orange Card, Carrs 188, etc) have melting points in the range 140–229°C; Perseverance special modelmakers' solder is 145°; and cast-kit solder, sometimes referred to as 'low-melt' or 'kit solder', melts at only 70°C.

In fact, this low-melt alloy is not strictly speaking a solder at all, although in practical terms it is used in the same way. It has far higher amounts of rare metals such as bismuth and antimony, a high proportion of tin, and is only compatible with lead-based alloys. In other words, it does not bond properly to brass, copper, nickel or steel, and is therefore not suitable to join these metals. The rule is that normal lead solders can be used both for 'hard' metals and for 'soft' lead-based castings, but not the other way about. The alloy we use to 'solder-assemble' our whitemetal kits is, in fact, a refined form of whitemetal itself; and the process may thus be considered more akin to welding than soldering.

As we noted in Chapter One, the greater the proportion of the rare metals in our whitemetal alloy, the higher the quality, the lower the melting point and the easier the flow characteristics. It's all to do with molecular structure and lattices and suchlike, but in practical terms it means that, carried further up the scale, our low-melt whitemetal alloy melts and flows at a temperature far enough below the melting-point of casting-grade alloy for that difference to be used to enable the castings to be joined without damage.

There's far more to it than that, however. We also need to understand the actual manner in which solders generally act, so that we can provide the ideal conditions for that action to take place. It is due to misunderstanding of these actions and reactions that most problems with soldering whitemetals arise.

CLEANSING & FLUXING

The first essential is to understand that solder joins by forming an actual mechanical bond with the metals to be joined. That is to say, the molecules on the surface of the molten mass of solder enter the molecular structure of the metal being joined, and 'link-up' with them, rather like Velcro. Obviously this cannot occur if the solder molecules can't actually get near the metal surface due to an overlying layer of grease and oxide! So we need to prepare the surface to receive the solder, by ensuring that the hapless molecules are laid bare. Mechanical surface cleaning with an abrasive such as a fibre-glass burnisher or wet-and-dry can help, although if the burnisher is soiled

from previous use as, say, a wheel or track cleaner, it will often put on more dirt than it removes!

Far more effective is chemical cleansing, generally by the action of an acid which will strip away the surface oxide of the whitemetal, taking the grease and dirt with it. In the case of our whitemetal (and almost all other modelling applications as well) the chemical we use is phosphoric acid, in a fairly dilute solution in water. This is sold by the trade (Eames '40', Model-Aids' Superflux) or can be readily obtained in hardware shops and chemists. 'Jenolite', a popular proprietary brand of rust-neutraliser for steel, is a fairly strong solution of phosphoric acid (it's pretty good at dealing with surface oxides generally). Jenolite, let down with about three times its own volume of distilled water, and with a dash of isy-propyl alcohol added as a wetting agent, makes an excellent flux, and is a lot cheaper than those soppy little bottles that are especially designed to fall over when you're in full flight with the soldering iron! You can also buy phosphoric acid from good dispensing chemists.

In point of fact, anything with phosphoric acid in it will do as a flux, including your favourite Cola (ugh, but handy if you run out on Sunday afternoon) even if the residue is a bit sticky!

HEAT TRANSFERENCE

The second major point that must be understood is the way in which heat travels through metals, and thus helps to melt them, or cause the molten metals to flow. The first essential is to get the heat out of the soldering-iron bit into the solder. When a metal is heated, the molecules become agitated, and start colliding, destroying the molecular structure which kept the metal rigid. Eventually, the structure collapses, and the metal melts. But, again, this will not happen if insufficient collisions take place — in other words, something else gets in the way, such as dirt or burnt flux on the face of the soldering iron, or, once again, grease and oxide on the metal surface. A clean iron, freshly tinned, will ensure that the solder melts readily and 'wets' the iron. Then, when it meets the surface of the metal to be joined, the clean surface will provide a ready path for the molecules to collide, the metal to heat, and the molten state of the solder to be maintained long enough for the molecular interaction to take place. A 'dry' iron gives a 'dry' joint, which means that, due to lack of molecular contact, the heat has not flowed and the overall 'joining-up' of the molecular structures has not taken place. Such a joint has little or no mechanical strength.

HEAT SOAK

Whitemetal, particularly the lower grades, is prone to a problem known as 'heat soak'. This is due to the lead in the alloy requiring a greater degree of 'excitement' than some of the flightier elements such as tin or antimony. Thus

the lead stays put when the other metals in the alloy are ready to 'go', preventing the heat-flow from spreading evenly and impeding the melting of the joining alloy — the solder. The trick is to go in with a sufficient reserve of heat energy to get the lead atoms on the move *tout de suite*, so that they don't hold up the other metals. In other words, a good soldering iron of adequate capacity — which will not be a knock-kneed tweeked-down 12V job with an output of only a few watts. A mechanical analogy — albeit a crude one — would be to consider trying to knock a hole in a wall by hitting it with a little hammer for a long time rather than taking one hefty swipe with a 12lb sledge! — with the ultimate conclusion that there are many occasions when you can peck away with your little hammer until doomsday without making any significant impression on the wall!

So it is with soldering, especially with those stodgy old lead atoms sitting in the whitemetal soaking up the heat of your little soldering iron while all the rest are dancing around. And then, all of a sudden, bingo! The lead moves, the other metals are already on the go, and you've got a hole in the casting before you can blink. And all the while the solder stays pasty and puddinglike on the bit and refuses to flow! Remember, too, that there is a time factor involved, that the transfer of heat is not instantaneous. So it follows, the longer it takes to get sufficient heat into the job, the longer that heat has to dissipate into the mass of the metal further and further from the point at which you're applying it (burning your fingers in the process, like as not). All of which delays — possibly fatally — the time at which the solder flows at the point of joining. Holding the job in your fingers is a good way of detecting the efficiency with which the process is taking place; the solder should run before you (expletive deleted) drop the whole issue!

SOLDER SUMMARY

I have dwelt at length on the detailed aspects of the soldering process, as once the whole thing is seen in a true light, a lot of the problems can be overcome. But the golden rules may be succinctly summarised as: cleaned, fluxed, fast-in, fast out with adequate iron. Not that this means some monster thing that takes half the output of the national grid to warm it up, weighs half a ton, and heats the entire house as well as the job in hand. Efficiency is the keynote, and there is no doubt that some soldering irons are a great deal more efficient than others. Where efficiency is combined with small size and light weight, we have the ideal iron for whitemetal kit assembly.

SOLDERING IRONS

A short aside on soldering irons is, perhaps, in order at this juncture. There are many different designs, but I have consistently found that irons with a fast recovery time are the most suited to modelmaking generally and kit assembly in particular. Recovery time? Well, consider our soldering iron, simmering away nicely with the bit at a temperature of X°. Along comes Joe modeller, and sticks the iron into some solder. (I know all the textbooks say you bring the solder and the iron to the job, but no modeller ever does or ever has done, unless he be very handy with his feet.) So heat travels from the bit, into the solder, which melts, and, hopefully, a good blob sticks to the bit. The element of the soldering iron now has to provide heat to replace that used in melting the solder, plus more heat to keep the solder molten. While the element is catching up, the bit is at a lower temperature than when it first made contact with the solder.

The iron is now introduced to a thumping great piece of metal, which, once contact is established, fairly sucks the heat out of the bit, which, naturally cools, maybe even to the point at which the solder freezes. The poor old element is by now panting away trying to restore the bit temperature, re-melt the solder, and get the metal up to a temperature at which the solder will flow. Obviously, the efficiency with which the element can do this will determine how long it is before the solder flows and the joint can be made.

There are a number of ways of overcoming this problem. The first is to have a very high-powered iron — which may overdo things, and get the whole issue too hot, too fast. The second is to have a very large bit, which contains such a vast reservoir of heat that coming into contact with the cold metals will not lower the temperature unduly. However, by its very nature such an iron will be large and unwieldy. Or we may provide an element of modest power, but ensure that the use of that power is optimised, by siting it close to the bit and giving it relatively little metal to heat. A valid analogy may be a car climbing a hill. A powerful engine will go up easily in top gear; a heavy car can take a run at it and get up on momentum; but a light car with a small engine and a good transmission will do just as well, probably on less fuel — that is, more efficiently.

In terms of soldering irons, those designs that use an element actually inside the bit provide that combination of efficiency and lightness that we require. Irons like the small Antex or the very similar SRB design lose little heat to the atmosphere, almost none to the handle. All the heat goes into the bit, and the path from element to bit to job is kept as short as possible. Hence the response time is fast, and these irons are equivalent to conventional (remote element) irons of twice the power. My own choice has been the SRB, which, like the Antex, has a range of readily interchangeable bits. I keep a separate bit for whitemetal work, as mixing 70° alloy and normal solders on one bit produces an unholy alloy of weird propensities and nil bond strength. Never pollute ordinary solders with 70°! This is not an expensive proposition, as a spare bit for the SRB Type 1 I use costs less than a pound.

The nominal rating of the iron is 18W, and I use a mains version at all times, although a 12V model is available — quite useful for wiring work on the car, but not really man enough for whitemetal. . . .

TEMPERATURE-CONTROLLED SOLDERING IRONS

These have long been associated with whitemetal kit assembly, and obviously have considerable advantage, provided that the temperature control is not associated with a lack of adequate power and the consequent lowering of efficiency. I have said that I do not like low-temperature irons, but I must qualify this. Could I but afford a really good low-temperature iron with a sensitive thermo-couple built into the tip and a feedback circuit controlling a power supply of adequate output so that the tip temperature would remain at the desired value, I should very much like to have one. But such an iron is a very professional piece of kit, and costs a very professional amount.

What I really do dislike is the common modeller's substitute for the true temperature-controlled iron, the tiny 12V turned right down on the output of a model railway controller, and for this reason. Typically, a small 12V iron is rated at 12–15W output. According to Ohm's law, therefore, if running at 12V, such an iron will draw a current of about 1 amp or a shade more. That is, more or less the full output of most model railway power packs. Turn the voltage down, however, and the current limitation of the power source will mean that the power of the iron will also be reduced more or less in line with the voltage. The 'adequate' 15W iron can only function as a feeble 6–9W device — with all the problems of inefficiency, lag and heat-soak already discussed as a consequence. If you want to use a 12V iron on a reduced voltage, you need a good hefty power supply of 2–2½ amps rating to keep the output at a decent level.

There is now a third alternative in the controlled-iron field, in the shape of the SRB soldering iron controller. This device is built into a case which plugs direct into a 13A 3-pin socket outlet, and is designed to substitute for the mains plug on the soldering iron. It will convert any mains-rated soldering iron up to an output of some 200W to a temperature-controlled iron, but without loss of power and efficiency. It is, in my view, a far superior alternative to the rather crude, bimetallic-strip type 'temperature controlled' irons which have been previously available. These, on the whole, are rather hit-and-miss affairs, tricky to adjust and somewhat inconsistent in operation. I never had much joy with them for whitemetal work.

The SRB controller is basically a variant of the familiarly thyristor lighting dimmer, and cuts output by 'chopping' parts of the AC cycle rather than reducing the actual power available. In use, one simply sets the control knob by trial and error (a use for scrap or discarded castings!) so that the soldering process is quick and efficient. If particularly large castings need to be joined, it is best to tweak the knob 'up' a notch or two, while delicate work may call for more reduction. I wired a wander-socket onto the output of my SRB controller, which enables me to plug in any of my various soldering irons for instant control. Obviously, with trial-and-error rather than an accurate temperature setting as the means of calibration, it is still not as satisfactory as the full professional job. But then, at less than twenty pounds, there are compensations. An SRB Type 1 iron and the SRB controller (now sold together as a 'whitemetal soldering outfit'), is probably the best bet for amateur whitemetal work.

SOLDERING IN PRACTICE

I hope by this stage you will have fought your way through my mish-mash of theory, opinion, fact and fancy, to some understanding of the soldering process. I also hope that you are encouraged rather than deterred! For it is really quite simple, not at all risky if the temptation to dwell be overcome, and a most speedy and satisfactory method of joining whitemetal castings. Obviously, if you're new to the game, it will pay to practise on some more modest model than a locomotive, and a road vehicle or wagon kit is a useful and economical way of gaining experience.

In my experience of running railway modelling courses, most of the problems that people experience with soldering whitemetal are due to timidity. That is to say, they use a weeny iron with insufficient capacity, and use it irresolutely, with the not surprising consequence that the heat transfer is too slow and inadequate to melt the solder, which refuses to flow, while the flux all boils uselessly away, reducing still further the efficiency of heat transfer. And so they sit there, prodding away with the warming-stick, more in hope than expectation, until they melt a hole or give up and go off looking for the Araldite.

My advocated approach is really the complete antithesis of this restrained delicacy. Slosh the flux on liberally, get a sufficiently hot iron with a nice big blob of molten solder balancing tremulously on the tip, and wallop it in with all the finesse of Frank Bruno landing a left hook. With the iron firmly in contact with the job and eyes streaming from the fumes of boiling flux, the misery is of short enduring as the solder melts and flows in a second or two. If it doesn't, off iron, re-flux (splosh it on like Henry Cooper with the Brut 33), back in again with a fresh blob of solder, and try again. Resist at all costs the lingering caress that may melt whitemetal faster than it melts the heart of your favourite lady.

A large part of the secret is the liberal use of the flux. Some people hoard the humble phosphoric as if it was 12-year-old single malt whisky. In addition to removing surface oxides, the boiling flux helps draw the molten solder into the surface, as well as into cracks

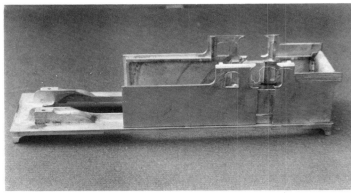
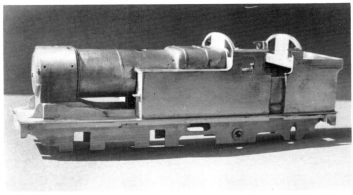

This is a typical assembly sequence for a whitemetal tank locomotive — the sidetanks and bunker are one-piece castings, erected onto the footplate with the bunker rear. Once these are square and secure, the rest of the superstructure is built into this 'shell'.

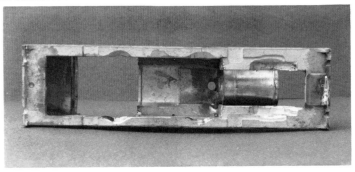

Here is the N7's scratchbuilt chassis, as yet devoid of detail. As soon as the basic body assembly was complete, trial-fitting to the chassis took place. And here is the result — the need to carve away quite a lot of metal from the underside of the footplate to give clearance for the coupling rods.

and crevices between the parts of the model. At any time when the soldering iron is in contact with the metal, there should be the merry hiss and tear-jerking fume of the acid vapourising. If it stops, you stop. Better to have too much than not enough (bit like the single malt, really . . .), as any excess is not inherently harmful, and is easily washed away with water. Do not worry, either, about the flux-staining, which tends to turn the model a dull grey. Leave this be, as it's in effect a primer, and forms an excellent basis for paint. In fact, I give completed whitemetal locos a thorough dose of flux before I paint 'em, rather in the way steel car-bodies are phosphate-dipped before spraying. Same process, effectively. Any 'free' acid is neutralised by standing the model in a bath of washing soda for half an hour before it is scrubbed for painting.

I'm also pretty liberal with the actual low-melt alloy itself. I like to fill cracks, holes, joints and so on, slightly proud of the surface of the casting so that I can use this as a reference for dressing-down with the scraper and abrasives. As the molten metal acts as a liquid, it forms a meniscus (curved concave edge) in angles or cracks. Also, being a hot metal, it shrinks slightly on cooling, so if you're a bit mean with the alloy it may shrink back and not fill the crack or what-have-you completely. That curved meniscus can be a giveaway in some situations, such as the footplate/cabside angle. I chase it out with a small screwdriver

stoned to a point, to give a nice crisp right-angle. In fact, with practice, you can persuade the alloy to do more or less what you want in terms of filling, although it will only 'bridge' relatively small holes or cracks — about ½ mm or so. If you have prepared your castings properly (and assuming that it's a reasonable kit in the first place), this takes care of most situations, and I usually reckon to do all my 'primary filling' with lowmelt alloy.

PATCHING

There are occasions when, for one reason or another, we are faced with the problem of restoring or making good damaged, melted or intentionally mutilated castings. Many people tend to throw up their hands (and throw in the towel) if the worst happens, and they melt a hole in the boiler or cabside. However, that which is melted out can also be melted back in! Faced with such an eventuality, it is quite possible to rebuild the casting by adding an 'intermediate' mix of metal, that is, an amalgam of scrap whitemetal and low-melt alloy, which will have a melting point somewhere between those of its constituents. This can be blobbed onto the damaged casting, a bit at a time, with plenty of flux to expedite the union, until there is sufficient metal to enable the casting to be filed, carved and papered back to shape.

Of course, you may lose a bit of detail doing this, which can either be accepted or reinstated,

using the techniques described in the next chapter. This approach can also be used for filling large, unwanted holes, left by the removal of inappropriate detail, or resulting from the relocation of a splasher, for instance. Here there are two refinements. One is to cut a blanking piece from scrap whitemetal sheet, which can be made by melting left-over odds-and-ends and pouring into a shallow container such as the lid of a tobacco tin. This blanking piece is then soldered in with the 70° alloy, and the joints finish-dressed as usual. Or, alternatively, a backing-piece of thin hard metal may be soldered behind the hole (see next chapter for soldering hard metals to whitemetal), and the hole filled by puddling in low-melt allow or alloy/whitemetal mix until a finish can be obtained. I have performed this surgery on many a Wills 'Hall', as instanced in Chapter One.

JIGS AND THINGS

Having dealt at great length with the means of joining the castings of our kit together, it now remains to look at the means by which these castings may be held in alignment whilst we are applying our glue or, more painfully, solder. Passing reference has been made to aids such as rubber bands and clothes-pegs, and there is no doubt that a suitable selection of similar helpmates can overcome the inherent difficulty of kit assembly: if the Good Lord had meant us to build 'em, we'd have four

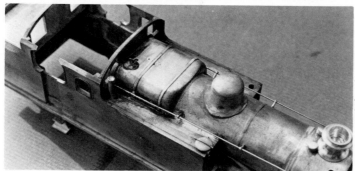
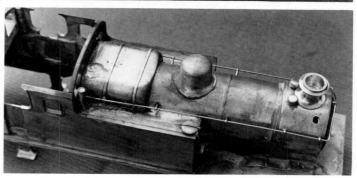

Disaster! A hole melted in the top of the N7's firebox! The underside view shows how a good quantity of a whitemetal/lowmelt mix has been 'puddled' into the hole, to give the basic 'stopping' visible in the third picture. The hole, now a mere crater, is then filled proud of the surface with lowmelt — though you could use filler — to give the result in the fourth picture, a simple dressing-down job with files and scraper, finished off with a wet-and-dry rubbing-stick. The last picture (below) shows the finished result, with the whistle hole re-drilled. Pity, that; I subsequently found it was in the wrong place!

hands, two at least fitted with heatproof fingers!

Reference is the first point—a reference surface from which to work, flat, true and big enough to stand the whole loco on. Plate glass is one option, or a good thick piece of Weyroc or similar. Mine is an offcut of kitchen worktop 1¼″ thick and surfaced with a smooth laminate. It's about 10″ x 4″, big enough for 4mm scale work. A nice refinement — which I may well get around to one day — is to mark a grid of squares on the working surface as an alignment aid. A selection of smaller blocks of Weyroc or hardwood are also useful for general propping-up and leaning-on purposes. A small (3″) engineers' square is also valuable for checking verticals.

To actually hold everything together whilst I ply the soldering iron, I have found Blu-tak to be invaluable. This is a sort of sticky putty which can be re-used umpteen times, and will hold quite well, although it works better on smooth, hard surfaces than absorbent ones such as wood. I generally find that between the bits of wood and the Blu-tak I can hold most castings in alignment long enough to make the soldered joint. Things need to be fairly firm, so that the iron can be applied with sufficient pressure to ensure good heat transfer.

Pressure is something often required for extended periods where glued assembly is contemplated. It can be applied in three ways — by using a spring or elastic material in tension, by adhesive tape or by weights. For assemblies like boilers, a couple of stout rubber bands

will hold all secure while the glue sets. Similarly, 'four-square' constructions like tender sides/top/footplate/frames can be 'rubber-banded' together, but do check that all is being held square before the glue goes off. Flat assemblies — tool-box or splasher to footplate, for instance — can be held with a spring clothes-peg or hair curler, both for soldering or gluing. Sidetanks or cabs can be weighted down onto footplates with a few chunks of heavy scrap, or even other parts of the kit.

Fortunately, many kits have alignment devices built into them, and so long as these do not conflict with the accuracy of the model, they should assist assembly. But do check, as they can sometimes throw the job out of kilter. Really, the whole matter of assembly comes down to improvisation and common sense. I

could write reams of suggestions, set-ups and scientific solutions to the problems that might be encountered, but it really all comes down to what is to hand when the occasion arises! Study of the photo-sequence accompanying these honeyed words of wisdom will show how I've gone about it for the 'guinea-pig' loco, but there will doubtless be equally valid alternatives. The only sure thing is that at some stage of the proceedings you will either get glue on the carpet or burn your fingers!

By now, our box of castings should be starting to bear some passing resemblance to the locomotive of which it is supposedly a model. It is time to start paying some attention to that which will give the model its final character and appearance — the detail. This is where the real fun starts!

CHAPTER FIVE
BASIC DETAILING

APPRAISAL
I suppose it is a not inappropriate juncture to trot out once more the keystone of kit construction as preached in these pages: appraisal, the frequent casting of the jaundiced eye. Self-criticism, quality control, satisfaction, regard it how you will, there is no escaping the fact that a model is either right, or it is not right. And, if the latter be the case, it must be put right, sooner rather than later.

So, just as we appraised the kit before purchase, again before preparation and assembly, it is well worth taking a good, hard look at the emergent model before putting long hours of delicate work into the detailing. What are we looking for? In a word, 'rightness'. Is the basic assembly square (it should be, if due care was taken in the assembling)? Does the boiler 'sit' properly in relation to footplate, splashers and cab? Is it parallel in both planes? Taper boilers are one thing, but inclined boilers only happen on funny Swiss engines for going up mountains.

And then, there are the finer points. Now that the model is 'in the round', how does the basic detail look? Is the beading too heavy, is it straight, is it parallel to the footplate? Are the cab windows right, do the spectacles relate properly in shape and position to the boiler? Does the cast cab-roof that you thought would be all right look so good now it's *in situ*? Or would a brass one look much better? Does all the cast-on detail line up as it should, or would it be better to scrape off that kinky vacuum pipe along the valances and replace it with a wire one that looks more capable of containing something so nebulous as nothing at all?

In other words, take a long, hard look at the model so far, and ask 'Am I satisfied with it, or could it be better?' Take it with you when you have your bath, prop it on the taps, and regard it thoughtfully as you soak. Only when you are convinced that, short of junking the whole issue and starting from scratch, what you have is as good as it's ever going to be — only then is it prudent to start in on the detailing. Once the model is festooned with a delicate tracery of handrails, pipework, lamp-irons and beadings, the chances of being able to take any major corrective action in respect of fundamental faults is reduced beyond the negligible, in spite of the slow-dawned sickening realisation that all is not well.

Also at this juncture, it is well to resolve any problems relating to the chassis, and the fitting thereof to the embryo superstructure. Quite apart from being easier to get at things when there is no detail to obstruct, the chance of being able to hold the model firmly enough to hack out clearances or remove enough metal

to lower the whole body a millimetre on the chassis is just about nil if the detail is to remain intact.

On the topic of locating the body on the chassis, a short aside. Do not attempt to join the two as though elemental forces are bidding fair to rend them asunder. A simple locating bracket at one end and a single fixing screw at the other is ample. After all, the object of the exercise is to ensure that the model stays in one piece when we pick it up. Super-rigid, multi-point screw fittings, all tightened up as if they were torque-loaded, do nothing more than distort the model (unless all the alignments are perfect, which mine never are!), and to make the thing a lot noisier by ensuring good transmission of noise and vibration from chassis to body.

Assuming that the model passes all these hurdles of perception and appreciation, we can at last get down to the most satisfying part of the process: adding the detail. This is the stage at which a normal, kit-built model can be given a real 'lift', taking it altogether out of the 'assembled kit' bracket.

RESTORING CAST DETAIL
The first stage of detailing involves work direct on the castings, rather than additions to them. We may need to restore rivets, beadings, pipework or other surface detail lost from the castings, either in the course of cleaning-up and assembly, or deliberately removed as unsatisfactory.

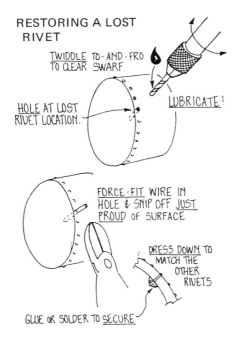

RESTORING A LOST RIVET

TWIDDLE TO-AND-FRO TO CLEAR SWARF.

HOLE AT LOST RIVET LOCATION.

LUBRICATE!

FORCE-FIT WIRE IN HOLE & SNIP OFF JUST PROUD OF SURFACE

DRESS DOWN TO MATCH THE OTHER RIVETS

GLUE OR SOLDER TO SECURE

Rivets are the commonest case in point, being frequent victims of the preparation stages. They can be revived by drilling a hole of suitable diameter at the rivet location, inserting and securing a length of appropriate wire, snipping off just proud of the surface, and dressing down to match the 'prominence' of the cast rivet detail. Sounds easy, and in truth it isn't difficult, just tedious, especially if you've a whole lot to do! Drilling the holes in whitemetal with small drills is a tricky business, though, as the drill is very apt to 'bind', usually with dire results! Apart from the not inconsiderable cost of repeatedly breaking small drills (and we are talking about 0.5 mm, number drills in the high 70s), one is left with the almost insoluble problem of bits of broken drill stuck firmly in the model. So, this is a circumstance to be avoided if at all possible.

Extreme care and delicacy is the approach. Forget all your labour-saving mini-drills, they'll bind and break a No. 78 drill in whitemetal before you can blink. Twiddle the drill in a pin-vice, in your fingers, to and fro. The back-twiddle will help to clear the drill, and a sensitive touch will tell you as soon as there is any suggestion of binding. If resistance increases, even very slightly, out drill (twiddling all the while), clear, re-lubricate, and try again. Lubrication? Yes, essential whenever you drill whitemetal. Not oil, which contaminates, but spit or soap, soft wax, glycerine, even liquid paraffin or petroleum jelly. Used carefully and properly lubricated, a small drill will last as well in whitemetal as in brass.

I like to force-fit the wire into the hole, which should be sufficient to retain it until the paint seals the whole job. This is also one application in which Cyano or Loctite 601 work well (exclusion of air in a good tight fit . . .). Soldering can only really be applied if the hole is drilled right through the whitemetal, and the solder applied from the back. I usually use brass pin wire and 145° solder for this work, remembering that the 70° cast-kit alloy does not bond well to hard metals. Once the wire is firmly in place, crop it off just proud of the surface with a good, sharp pair of side-cutters, file the end down to the right height for the rivet, and round off with fine wet-and-dry on a stick.

SOLDERING HARD METALS TO WHITEMETAL
Almost all other detail work from this point on will involve the soldering of detail fabricated in brass, nickel-silver, copper or steel to the basic whitemetal kit assembly. In my experience the 70° low-melt alloy we have been using to join our castings together is not

suited to these hard metals, so we have two alternatives; to use a normal solder, which will bond both to the brass and to the whitemetal; or to interpose a layer of lead-based alloy on the surface of the hard metal, and then to use the 70° alloy to do the actual joining.

Of these two alternatives (I'm ignoring glued methods here as the techniques will not differ from the basic kit assembly), my own preference lies with the former. The solder I use for this work is one of the low-melt 'conventional' solders, such as the Brewster's Orange Card or Perseverance Modelmakers, both of which melt at 145°. Again, provided that you observe the rules and precautions applied when soldering the whitemetal castings together, no problems should arise. Obviously, it is far safer to apply the soldering iron to the hard metal rather than the casting, as apart from the hazards associated with applying soldering irons in general to whitemetal castings, the hard metal will conduct heat far more efficiently than the lead-based castings, and the joint will be completed quicker and consequently at less risk.

When the 'hard' component to be joined is large — a cab roof, for instance, or a smoke deflector — then it may not always be possible to run a seam joint as might be made if it were a whitemetal-to-whitemetal joint with 70° alloy, in which case, there are two options. Tack the components together with the 145° solder, to provide the mechanical strength, and then run the seam in 70°. It won't give a strong bond, but no matter, as the joint has already been secured. Or recourse may be had to method number two, the 'tin-and-seam' approach. (If you're brave and deft, it is possible to flow a seam in 145° between brass and whitemetal — a hot, clean iron and plenty of flux, lots of solder to conduct the heat, and don't linger . . .)

'Tin-and-seam' is self-explanatory. The 'hard' metal is first tinned with an ordinary lead-based solder, and here we ideally need one with a high melting point. The tinned hard metal and the whitemetal can now both be treated as whitemetal, and the joint made with 70° alloy. Why the high-melt tinning? As pre-

viously remarked, if 70° alloy and normal lead-tin solders are mixed, the resulting concoction is a nasty, solder-like alloy with very poor bonding ability to hard metal (no better, in fact, than the 70° alloy, which seems to 'infect' the solder). To prevent this happening, we need to tin our hard metal with a solder that isn't going to melt and mix with the 70° alloy when we make the joint. I use Multicore 50/50 tinman's solder (green and red pack) for tinning, and I also use separate irons (or bits) for the two types of solder.

It does not need much deep thought to see that one or other of these two techniques can be used to add all the detail to our whitemetal locomotive body, that is, where a permanent joint is required. For components that may need to come off — for painting, perhaps — it may behove us to consider a mechanical fixing such as screwing, force-fit, pinning, riveting or splayed fit. But for the nonce, I intend to consider soldered detail, and the best materials and means of making and fixing same.

BEADING
In the good old days, beadings were always made out of fuse-wire. This, however, has a number of drawbacks. It is tinned copper wire, which conducts heat very readily, making soldering a bit tricky — the heat runs away down the wire, and the whole thing is apt to race up to joining temperature rather than just the bit required. Also, when cleaned up, fuse-wire beading is copper, whereas most prototype beading was brass. And nothing looks more like brass than brass. The other main drawback of fusewire is its softness, which makes it very difficult to obtain nice, straight, even beading. It also comes in a limited range of thicknesses.

I prefer brass wire for beadings, especially the fine pin-wires sold by Alan Gibson in diameters from 0.32 mm (about a scale 1 inch) upwards. This comes drawn and straight, and, being hard, stays that way. For long runs of beading such as tender-tops, sidetanks or cabs, it lies flat and true unless a bend is deliberately applied. For more intricate, curvy beadings — splashers, spectacles and suchlike — I prefer fine soft brass wire sold for use in the making

of silk flowers. (Try your local refined handicrafts shop.) This is very malleable, but does not break easily. It is usually of 0.4 mm diameter, just right.

Soldering beadings onto whitemetal castings is without doubt one of the trickiest operations in the whole detailing process. Which is why, I suppose, most kits have the beading cast in, hopefully in a form in which it can be retained without looking too bad. But there is no doubt

Alan Ketley's 'Merchant Navy' in the raw. To achieve this standard, many hours have gone into the preparation and refinement of DJH's excellent castings.

that brass splasher beading, for instance, can look the bee's knees, and I often rate it worth the trouble of scraping off the cast beading and replacing it. I use a hot, clean iron, the 145° solder (not too generously this time if you don't want a lot of difficult cleaning up) and plenty of flux.

If it is possible to anchor one end of the beading by tack-soldering on the back of the

job, life is a lot easier. This is usually just a matter of drilling a small hole—in the case of splashers, through the footplate. I always pre-tin beading wire with 50/50 solder as a precaution — it means I can use either method of soldering. Then I poke one end of the wire through my anchor-hole, and solder it firmly in place (i.e., a good blob!). With one end as a 'datum', I now work my way along the beading, making tiny tack-joints at intervals, especially changes in direction. Lots of flux — I keep stressing this, it's the key to success — and the tip of the hot iron with a wee droplet of solder serves to secure the beading to the whitemetal. You will now have a wire with a series of 'full-stops' strung along it. Re-flux, and, working in random order, touch the clean iron to the wire adjacent to each tack. The tiny blob will melt and the solder runs in behind the wire. Perfect!

Any 'gaps', where the beading is not soldered to the casting, can be 'touched-in' with 70° alloy, but try to avoid melting the alloy and the 145° together if possible. Once the wire is firmly soldered in place, any necessary

cleaning up can be carefully undertaken with scraper, sharpened screwdriver and abrasives. I also file the face of the beading flat, baring the underlying brass to convince all and sundry that it isn't a cast-kit model at all. . . .

I often adopt a similar approach to cabside cut-outs, except that instead of soldering wire to the face of the casting I solder flat strip into the actual opening in the cabside. (This last will, of course, have been thinned down to near-scale thickness when the castings were being prepared . . .) The strip I use is waste from etched kit frets, a most invaluable detailing material. Fine brass strip, about 8–10 thou thick and in widths from 0.8 mm up, would be a useful addition to the materials available from the trade. If you have access to a good-quality guillotine, fine strips can be cropped from 10 thou hard brass sheet, otherwise a bit of scrounging is in order — you must know someone who builds etched kits!

Once again, I fix one end securely, tack round the opening from the inside of the cab,

The BR 2—6—4T has all the normal varieties of handrail — in stanchions on the boiler, grab-irons on the bunker rear and vertical standards at the cab doorway.

re-flux, and run the solder into the joint by re-melting. In this case, the back of the strip only needs to be tinned. In fact, these cabside beadings are one of the instances when the tin-and-seam approach works very well indeed. And, once more, it is one of those 'hi-fi' touches that set a model apart.

The last type of beading that often benefits from replacement is that along the top of tender-sides. This is much easier than beading soldered flat to a face or into an opening, as the joint is 'open' to the soldering-iron. I usually seam these beadings straight off; tin the wire, tack one end, load the iron with the chosen type of solder, apply plenty of flux, and draw the iron steadily along the joint. Working from the top of the job, the molten solder can be fed directly into the gap between wire and whitemetal, and a neat, clean job results. All highly satisfactory. Once again, I square the beading up with a file, unless the prototype had the half-round variety (LNER group standard tenders, for instance).

HANDRAILS

Nothing lets down the look of a model locomotive more than handrails that are too heavy, wonky, out-of square or exhibiting non-prototype kinks and curves. Matters have improved a very great deal in recent years with the arrival on the market of decent, near-scale handrail knobs available in a variety of lengths. My own pet hate was the 'row of footballs on a water-main' look that has typified kit-built models. The other great giveaway has been the 'one-length disease', when the handrail dived in and out from smokebox to boiler and back out to firebox because the handrail knobs were all the same length and did not allow the variety of spacing used to keep prototype handrails straight. Allied to this unwanted wandering has been the 'shiny gas-pipe' appearance of bright nickel-silver wire, usually of a diameter about 2½ times scale.

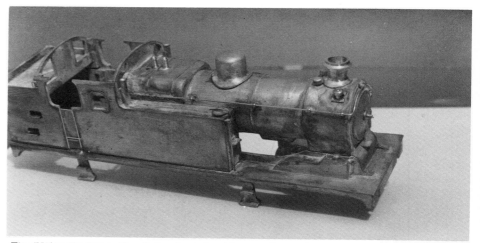

The 'N7' boiler handrails call for short stanchions on the smokebox and long ones on the boiler. I have used Alan Gibson's turnings, available in three lengths.

A prototype handrail is typically from 1¼ in– 2½ in in diameter; that is, represented in 4 mm scale by wire from 0.45 mm–0.7 mm. It will not have escaped your notice that these two diameters, along with 0.33 mm (scale 1 inch) are available in brass pin-wire, which is an eminently suitable material for making handrails, being hard, straight and inclined to stay so. Used in conjunction with knobs made to suit, either turned or closed-down splitpins, this wire will make really true, fine handrails that will again set a model apart from the clumsy, over-heavy look for so long associated with whitemetal. Both wire and turned knobs (more properly, stanchions), in three lengths, are available from Alan Gibson.

A study of prototype photographs will quickly show that the vast majority of locomotives had their handrails painted over, either in the base livery colour or in black. It is only the older locos that tended to have burnished handrails, but these were, of course, steel. Which is how I choose to represent them, by

using steel piano wire, available in a number of suitable diameters from your local model aeroplane shop. The only drawback to this wire is that it is difficult to bend, being very hard indeed. To overcome this problem, I anneal the wire at those points where I wish to bend it, by heating it to red heat in the blowlamp. (If you haven't a blowlamp, a candle-flame is surprisingly effective.)

I have never had any joy whatsoever trying to make handrails — which are, as noted, predominately straight — out of nickel-silver wire sold in coils — which is utterly and irredeemably curved — or from some of the soft and soggy wires reputedly supplied for the purpose. It is a lot easier to put an accurate bend into hard, straight wire than it ever is to straighten soft or curved wire. And I'm all for the easy life. . . .

Bending handrails to shape is a nice art — and art it is, for science is of little aid. As with so much in the construction of model locomotives, it's a case of suck-it-and-see, trial the error. Sophisticated technical types call it fitting. I prefer to regard it as refined bodging. The worst handrail is the most common, the one that goes down one side of the boiler, up around the front of the smokebox, and back down the other side, all in one go as far as the model is concerned, although on the prototype it's actually three sections, joined in the stanchions on the side of the smokebox. I've tried to achieve this joint, but in a 4 mm scale knob that's anywhere near a reasonable size, it's well-nigh impossible. In 7 mm scale, it can be done.

Faced with such a handrail, I start by making the curved section at the front of the smokebox. Then, not forgetting to thread on a knob for the centre-top of smokebox location, I form the bends to take the handrail round onto the smokebox sides, and end up by cropping each end to length to suit the boiler. In other words, I start from the middle and work outwards. Apart from all else, it's a lot easier to make the curved sections on the front of the smokebox — very visible on the finished model — nice and symmetrical working 'in the flat' on the bench, rather than trying to fiddle it *in situ*.

Fitting boiler handrails is yet another of those operations that are greatly simplified if the boiler/smokebox/firebox can be kept as a separate sub-assembly. If the handrail stanchions have sufficiently long tails — one reason I still like to represent them with splitpins — then they can be soldered in place from the rear, by poking the soldering iron carefully down from the firebox end. A classic failing of many whitemetal kits is to have massive holes cast into the boiler to take the handrail stanchions — which usually fit with a scale 3 in clearance all round! The only remedy is to fill these holes with either whitemetal/70° alloy mix or Milliput, and re-drill at a more reasonable size. It's well worth making handrail stanchions a good fit, so I drill undersize and carefully open out the holes with a taper brooch (lubricate!) until the tail of the stanchion will just enter the front of the hole. This means that the stanchion can be pushed home when the time comes, and will stay put until secured.

I have sometimes seen advocated the practice of leaving the fitting of handrails until the painting is completed — a device beloved of the bright gas-pipe brigade. This has never struck me as a good idea — there seems far more risk of damaging the paint finish when trying to fit handrails than there ever is in cleaning wayward paint from rails already *in situ*. It also restricts the means by which the handrails may be secured, as soldering a painted loco seems fraught with hazards. And I do prefer to solder handrails wherever practicable as they tend to get handled a lot when the model is complete, and thus need to be as strong as possible.

Once I have bent my boiler handrail to shape, fitting is a matter of threading on the appropriate number and type of stanchions for each side of the boiler (typically: 1 or 2 short on smokebox; 3 long on boiler; 1 or 2 medium or short on firebox — hence the need for different knobs) and, starting from the front, 'springing' the rail at each side to allow the foremost stanchions on the smokebox to be entered into their holes (it may pay to shorten the tails of these two, especially if you're using splitpins). It is then best to work back symmetrically on both sides of the boiler, pushing the tails of the stanchions home in those nice, tight holes. It will also simplify matters if the handrail is eased out at the smokebox end — I usually work with the rail as far out as possible, so that the 'cab-ends' of the rail are just in the rearmost knob on each side. This gives the rail a lot more 'spring', and makes it easier to get the tricky smokebox-side stanchions in place. Once all the stanchions, except the smokebox front one, are pushed home, the rail is eased back, working each side alternately a few mm, until the front stanchion can be entered in its hole atop the smokebox door.

At this juncture, I usually secure the rearmost stanchions on both sides — nice and easy to solder from the back with a touch of 145°. I also secure the rail to these stanchions — check that the smokebox-front section is nice and symmetrical, and evenly-spaced from the front of the smokebox. These two stanchions, plus the one on the smokebox front, give the three datums which determine the 'sit' of the handrails. Check carefully that the rail is parallel to the footplate — if it isn't, now is the time to adjust matters, by either easing the rear knobs or juggling the front one up or down a fraction. The rear is easier to adjust, as it will not affect the curve of the rail over the smokebox door.

Once the ends of the rail are all secured in the correct relationship, the chances are the 'straight' sections down the side of the boiler are as full of kinks as an Irish back-road. Sight along each rail, and carefully 'tweak' the stanchions up or down a fraction until the alignment is true. (This assumes that you've drilled the holes pretty much in a straight line ... but you checked that long before trying to fit the rails, did you not?) Once the rail is truly aligned, parallel both to the boiler and to the footplate, free of kinks and generally looking right, it may be finally secured. I do not find it behoves me to fix at each and every stanchion — I usually content myself with the three 'anchor points' and one stanchion about the middle of each boiler-side. The rest should stay put of their own volition, helped perhaps by a tiny spot of loctite or cyano if the soldering iron won't reach. If you find that you need to solder on stanchions from outside the boiler, a neat dodge is to tin the tails with 50/50 tinman's solder, then countersink the holes in the boiler, and fix with 70° alloy — which fills the countersink flush instead of forming a hard-to-clean-off blob at the base of the stanchion.

I've dealt at great length with the fitting of boiler handrails, as, to judge from many of the models that I've seen over the years, it is an operation which gives a lot of people problems, especially where they are trying to work with over-thick, unco-operative wire that came off a coil, in sloppy-fitting knobs located in holes several sizes too large. . . .

Cabside handrails and the assorted grab-irons dotted about the nether end of locomotives are nowhere near such a problem. If

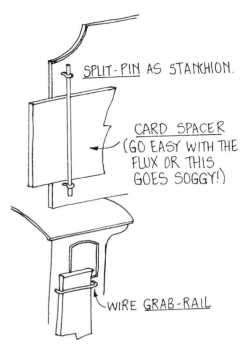

SPLIT-PIN AS STANCHION.

CARD SPACER (GO EASY WITH THE FLUX OR THIS GOES SOGGY!)

WIRE GRAB-RAIL

USING SPACERS TO SET HANDRAILS

turned stanchions are being used, then the matter is simplicity itself; thread stanchions onto a suitable piece of wire, locate in nice tight holes drilled in cabside, tender or bunker; solder from rear, and snip off excess wire. Where split-pins are being used, or grab-rails fitted, then a scrap of card of suitable thickness may be used to ensure accurate spacing.

This only leaves the vertical stanchions fitted at cab doorways, tender platforms and at the front of sidetanks. Strictly speaking, these should be slightly tapered, but just thinking about the turnery involved to make them gives me bright lights behind the eyes, so I use wire and imagine the taper. The anchorage for the top of these stanchions is almost always formed from the continuation of a beading, either that of the cabside cut-out, or the top bead of tankside or tender. If you've added beading, then it's no problem to make allowance for these stanchions, but most kits don't. The alternatives are either to put a right-angled bend in the top of the stanchion, and solder to cabside or whatever is appropriate. The other, nicer, solution is to put a small 'u' in the end of a piece of fine wire (fuse wire), and to solder

*Pipework and handrails as they should be, on another
Alan Ketley masterpiece, the BR '9F' 2—10—0 in 18.33, from a DJH kit.*

CABSIDE HANDRAIL STANCHIONS

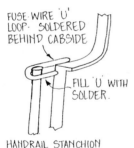

this both to stanchion and to cabside, making sure that the 'u' is filled with solder. This dodge is also used for the mid-point fixing on those tender engines that have a rear-of-cab stanchion extending from footplate to cab roof. In all cases, the foot of the stanchion is secured in a hole drilled in the footplate.

PLUMBING

Plumbing and handrails are, from the model-making point of view, more or less the same thing. The only real difference seems to be that the kit manufacturers never try and cast the former, but always try and cast the latter! The result is usually a wonky, malformed, fragile and flashridden excrescence that looks like a python with bad indigestion. I bin all such offerings, for the fabrication of vacuum pipes, lubricator runs, injectors, ejectors, clack-

valves and feed-pipes in wire, washers, bits of brass capilliary tube and small nuts is both simple and satisfying.

In the photographs and sketches I illustrate the methods of forming the most common fittings that adorn steam locomotives. Fittings so produced will be neater, crisper, closer to scale and altogether superior to any cast contortions. Not only that, where a pipe on the prototype is copper or brass duly burnished, it can be likewise brazen or cuprous upon the model. All that is needed is a selection of copper and brass wires of differing diameters. Conveniently, the bigger pipes were usually copper (feeds, injectors, etc.) and can conveniently be represented by solid copper wire from mains cable, available in cross-sections from $0.75 \, mm^2$ upwards. Standard 5 amp lighting ring cable gives a nice scale 2¼ in diameter pipe, just the job for the feeds to boiler clack valves.

Brass pipes, on the other hand, were less common, and usually small bore. Which means that the old standby, the brass pin wire, can be pressed into service once more. Other small pipes, such as lubricator feeds, can be represented by 5 amp fusewire, or, where really fine, by single strands of copper wire taken from flex. It is well worth adding these small pipes, as they can add much to the subtle character of a model. Where the pipes follow an intricate path, as in the case of many oil feeds, the thin copper wires are very easy to manipulate.

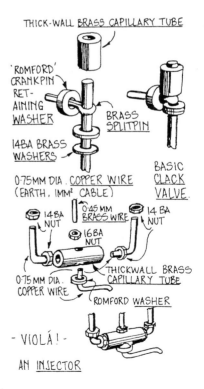

DETAILS FROM WIRE, WASHERS AND WHATNOT

Thin copper wire — usually five-amp-fuse — has another important role in the modelling of plumbing, for it is the ideal means of attachment. A short length is looped around the pipe to be mounted, and the tails twisted together. A dab of flux and a touch of the soldering iron with a spot of 145° will secure to the pipe, and render the tail quite strong enough to be fed through an appropriate hole drilled in the model, where it can be secured behind in the approved manner. Of course, if your preferences lie that way, all this securing work, for both handrails and for pipework, can be accomplished with adhesives. And, if the point about making the locating holes drilled in the whitemetal has been duly taken, then cyano-acrylate will give a strong and unobtrusive bond. Just try not to glue your fingers on at the same time. . . .

Very small pipes, however, do not lend themselves to attachment by twisted-fusewire brackets. The bracket tends to end up as hefty as, or heftier than, the pipe. Here, I solder the pipe on directly, exactly as I have described for beadings, except that I just tack in sufficient places to retain the pipe, rather than trying to 'seam' along the whole length. Again, a hot, clean iron, a good dollop of flux, and a tiny drop of solder on the tip of the bit—and it's surprising how easily and neatly these small but essential details can be fixed. I find that 145° solder serves me best, as it's less inclined to whizz off hither-and-thither than is the capricious 70° alloy.

SECURING PIPEWORK

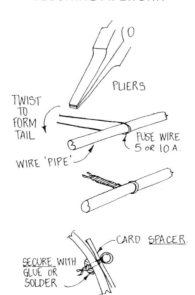

PLIERS

TWIST TO FORM TAIL

WIRE 'PIPE'

FUSE WIRE 5 OR 10 A.

CARD SPACER.

SECURE WITH GLUE OR SOLDER

LAMP-IRONS

There is no getting away from the fact that fitting convincing, robust lamp-irons to a whitemetal locomotive is a bit of a job. The 'straight' variety are bad enough, but those GWR efforts with a left turn half-way are the devil incarnate, occasioning as they do a deal of profanity. I make my lamp-irons from the fine brass fret-waste already noted as a good source for flat beadings. I have also used some fine phosphor-bronze strip about ½mm wide, sold for pick-ups (for which it was far to insubstantial). But there is no doubt that some nice, parallel, thin (about 8 thou) brass or nickel strip would be most useful in the production of lamp-irons that were somewhere near scale.

Lamp-irons are amongst the most fragile and vulnerable detail on a model locomotive, and for this reason it is wisest to wait until almost all other work has been completed before fitting them. It is also essential to make sure that they are well-secured, otherwise the pre-paint clean-up will inevitably dislodge them. There is no substitute for solder in the secure attachment of tiny bits like these — but on the other hand, they're the very devil to solder on! The secret is, of course, not to part the lamp-iron from the rest of the strip until after the joint is made.

Leaving aside those GWR oddities for the moment, lamp-irons come in two basic forms. The simplest is just a vertical strip, the lamp itself sitting on the footplate. Where the bracket is elevated — smokebox front, bunker or tender rear — then the lamp sits on a projecting tongue which is part of the iron itself. There are also nasties like combined lamp-irons and destination board brackets, but they are really just more of the same, and no worse than the GWR efforts.

The basic 'L-iron' is not difficult to make — just take your strip and turn the last mm or so neatly round through 90° to form the foot of the 'L'. I find I can sweat these direct to the footplate using the 145° solder, tinning the base of the 'L' and applying the iron to the topside of the tinned member, remembering, of course, that a 'dry' iron (no solder on the bit) will not transfer heat, and that adequate flux is needed to ensure that the solder flows. Whilst all the hot stuff is going on, you have the remainder of the strip to hold, which, hopefully, shouldn't get too warm. Once the joint is firmly made — check by a robust tug on the strip — the excess can be snipped of and *voila*! One lamp-iron. A nice touch is to very gently round the top of the iron with fine abrasive on a rubbing-stick.

The alternative soldering method of tinning with 50/50 tinman's solder and joining with 70° low-melt alloy can also be used, but I find it not as strong and more likely to result in an unsightly blob of metal at the foot of the iron. One further alternative is to make two right-angle bends, to give a 'tail' to pass down into a hole drilled in the footplate. This can be tinned, and the soldering done below the footplate.

Where lamp-irons need to be attached in elevated locations, then the 'tail-in-hole' method is usually the best. I usually drill the hole undersize, and crunch the 'tail' of the lamp-iron into a sort of square-section in the pliers. The hole is then eased out with the taper-brooch until the tail of the iron just enters, when it can be soldered or even glued into place. The irons themselves need a little more forming, and I start by making an 180° fold with fine snipe-nose pliers, crimping this flat. I then turn up the long end of the strip some ½mm from the nose of the fold to give the actual lamp bracket, and make a corresponding and opposite fold a further ½mm in to form the 'tail'.

And now for those GWR brackets. I cheat on these, and make the necessary 90° bend by folding the strip over on itself and crimping

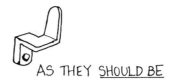

AS THEY SHOULD BE

FOLD OVER

RICE'S COMPROMISE

GW LAMP-IRONS

flat, which gives a neatly-mitred (but unproto-typical) corner. I then turn up bracket and turn down tail as before. The subterfuge is not too noticeable, and as the only alternative is to start fretting out tiny 'L' strips (or buying etched ones from such as Crownline), which are very difficult to solder in place, I prefer not to look too closely. Of course, the GWR footplate brackets are no more difficult than any others, merely 90° out of phase.

I have found that all basic detail can be represented by one or other of the processes described in this chapter; wire-in-hole for rivets and bolts; sweated-on wire and strip for beadings; wire in stanchions, split-pins or fusewire brackets for pipes and handrails; and strip sweated on or fitted in holes for lamp-irons. Where the ingenuity has to start is when we have to start grafting in replacement parts, additional sheetwork or turned or cast fittings — another part of the 'refining' process that started at the casting-preparation stage.

M & L 'Manor' with the full panoply of refinements, once again applied by Alan Ketley. GW lamp irons from strip, lubricator pipework from wire. Smokebox door darts and buffers are turnings.

CHAPTER SIX

GILDING THE LILY

Back in the old days of the 'blind eye' convention, when no one expected a model locomotive (other than those by Beeson, Miller-Swan or Mike Longridge) to possess any more in the matter of detailing than was strictly necessary to enable the prototype of the model to be recognised with reasonable surety, there arose the term 'superdetailed'.

A superdetailed locomotive was one which actually went so far as to represent other than this most basic detail. Add on a full complement of handrails, the odd bit of plumbing and — dizzy height of fidelity — a lamp-iron or two, and the proud owner would assert that this was, indeed, a superdetailed model. Never mind the cab full of motor, the lack of daylight under the boiler, the unadorned bullhead rail masquerading as coupling rods and the rudimentary valve gear — there was a vacuum pipe on the front beam, was there not? And then there came builders such as Alan Taylor and Guy Williams, producing locomotives that were not only correct in all basic essentials, but also carried such unheard of refinements as brake and sanding gear, cab fittings, lubricators, injectors, correct pipework, washout plugs, full rivet detail, fall-plates, water-scoops on the tender and actually had glazing in the cab spectacles. Objects of wonder, indeed, regarded with awe, envy and amazement by all who beheld them.

But what of today? In front of me as I write stands a model of LMS 5XP No. 5700 *Amethyst*. It is 4mm scale, 00 gauge. The wheels are correct in diameter, have the appropriate number of spokes, with accurately modelled bosses and balance weights. The coupling rods are close to scale, fluted, and have boss and oil-box detail. The Walschaerts valve-gear makes few concessions to the exigencies of the modeller's art. The correctly-detailed cylinders have drain cocks, a nice representation of the valve-spindle brackets, correct rectangular-section slidebars and the right design of crosshead. There is full brake gear, sandboxes and sandpipes. Above the footplate, the locomotive is beautifully modelled and incorporates all the prototype's rivet detail, beadings, washout-plugs, top-feed, lubricators, sandbox fillers, handrails and grab-irons, vacuum ejector, reversing rod and brackets, cab-roof vent, rainstrips, even lifting rings and drag beam detail. The cab has interior detail, and the windows are glazed. The tender, too, is superbly rendered, with full drag-beam and shovelling-plate detail, brake and scoop standards, coal rails (about the weakest feature on the model — they are too thick and heavy), vents, filler, dome, water scoop, beadings, rivets, brake gear, correct buffers, even the builder's plate on the rear.

Who is responsible for this paragon of the miniature loco-builder's art? A veritable championship winner, the envy of all and the preserve of the rich or talented? Not a bit of it — Mainline, made in Hong Kong, available from your local model shop for roughly the price of a medium-sized whitemetal kit. I've got one of those, too. I won't name names, but it is an 0–6–0 tender engine. The wheelbase is wrong, the driving wheels are the wrong size, there is no brake gear, although there

'Amethyst', the arbiter. This Mainline Jubilee sits on my workshop shelf to remind me what the current R-T-R baseline is — horribly good!

are a couple of sandboxes, praise be! The (etched) chassis has massive cut-outs to accommodate the motor, which also blocks the daylight under the boiler and obstructs the cab. The chassis does not extend for the full length of the loco, and there is also a very nasty gap where it fails to meet the running plate.

Above the footplate, matters are a little better. There is a fair amount of detail, not very crisp, but the boiler fittings are accurate and look the part. The cab roof is totally wrong, and lacks ventilator and rivet detail. There is no cab interior of any sort, no proper drag beam, not even a cab floor. The front bufferbeam is devoid of rivet detail, has the wrong type of buffer cast integrally with it, has no provision for scale couplings and only a crude, fragile vacuum pipe. The handrails are the wrong shape, far too thick and are held in knobs resembling footballs. There is some pipework, a very crude representation of a lubricator, and some sandbox fillers, but no reversing gear of any sort!

The tender is to much the same standard, and has incorrect steps and filler. Again, there is no underframe detail, and the wheels supplied are the wrong type and the wrong diameter. A lot of the detail, such as the brake standards and filler, is crude and inaccurate. The handrails are overscale and the wrong type. And as for a builder's plate . . .

The intention of this lengthy diatribe is to point up the regrettable fact that a very great many — though by no means all — the white-metal locomotive kits on the market today are far more reminiscent of the standards of twenty years since, rather than those of today as embodied in the excellent Mainline 'Jubilee'. And it is my contention that our kitbuilt loco, to be worth building in the first place, must be at least as good as a ready-to-run equivalent. So how can we make up the deficiency?

In the last chapter, we dealt with the basic detailing of the model. Much of this will, hopefully, have been incorporated in the kit, in such a way that it can be accepted 'as is', or modified to a suitable standard. Mention has also been made along the way of the substitution of scratch-built or bought-in items for the less successful cast components of the kit. This is the process which can now be taken a step further. The time has come to cast out compromise, and to undo that which heedless moulders of metal would have us do.

There are a number of aspects to be looked at in this final stage of the refining process. The first, and most important, is to minimise the intrusion of the motor into those places where prototype locomotives, if they wear anything, certainly do not sprout whirring armatures and massive chunks of magnetised steel. But what of the boiler with a quarter of its circumference missing, the firebox with no front, or the cab with no floor? We must branch out, perchance, into a little mild scratchbuilding, and provide these desirable addenda for ourselves.

This is by no means as daunting a prospect as it might seem, for we have already covered the trickiest part of the process, the joining of hard-metal components to the whitemetal castings. All that is usually required is some thin metal, a pair of snips or scissors, and the odd file or two. Brass of 10 or 15 thou thickness in a softish to half-hard grade will serve, and is easily worked. Basically, all the components we will need to produce are either flat plates, or simple cylindrical curves.

BOILER FILLETS

Bottomless boilers are a particular *bête noire* of mine, and I find it worthwhile to take considerable trouble mending these holes. They are, fortunately, usually simple rectangles in plan, which obviates any fancy fitting. I cut a piece of softish brass to the right length, but a few mm too wide. I then curve this to as

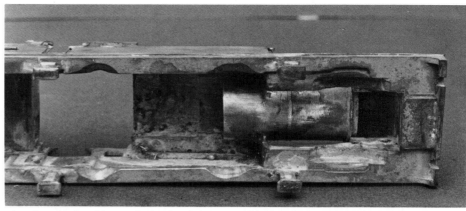

Another classic whitemetal kit giveaway is the boiler which, very obviously, stops short at the tank front. Here, I have remedied this by soldering a bit more boiler (a spare whitemetal casting from the N7 kit) onto the rear of the main boiler, to give the illusion of continuity.

FILLING IN BOILER CUT-OUTS

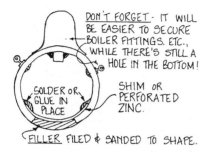

near the same radius as the boiler as I can get, although it is surprisingly uncritical. The ideal way of curving sheet like this is to use a rolling mill, but in the entirely likely circumstance of this rather specialised tool being absent, it can be managed quite readily by using a piece of dowel as a former. This needs to be a bit smaller in radius than the desired boiler plate, to allow a bit of spring. I find that I can get most boiler curves using a bit of ⅝ in ramin dowel and my fingers.

Once a suitable curve has been imparted to the metal, it is simply a case of carefully trimming with snips and files until it just fits the hole, a bit at a time, and keep offering up, checking, and back for another pass of the file. The essential thing about this fitting process is to achieve a fit — and you're very unlikely to do that by measurement, though it's surprising how many people try! It is a proficient modeller indeed who can measure, mark, cut and file to an accuracy much better than about plus or minus 0.5mm. And that's a scale 1½ in crack in the boiler!

Once the fill-in plate has been made, it is located and soldered in place. The tin-and-seam method is probably easier in this instance, and it will do no harm if the solder ends up a bit proud of the joint. A modicum of dressing with scraper, files and emery boards will produce a joint that, with a touch of finish-filling, will disappear beneath the paint.

All this, of course, assumes that the boiler-bands have been removed, and that the boiler is still separate from the footplate to facilitate operations.

There is an effective alternative to the metal fillet, and that is to insert a backing piece

behind the hole, and then make good with filler. A piece of thin brass soldered in place, or even some of that perforated zinc they give you with car body repair kits, will allow filler such as Plastic Padding type elastic or, best of all, Milliput, being applied. Once this has cured, it can be dressed to the curve of the boiler with files and abrasives (remember the flat backing!).

CAB INTERIORS

Cab floors are another component often sacrificed on the altar of unsubtle motor mounting. Even if there is some unavoidable intrusion into the cab of magnet or gears, it is still possible to fit a floor around or over it. This is particularly true of tank engines, many kit-built specimens leaving the driver to stand on thin air! And nothing is a surer giveaway than daylight showing through where the floor should be. If the intrusion into the cab is merely a

gearset, it is often possible to lose this by either setting the floor a few mm too high, or by tilting it to clear the worm.

The making of the actual floor is simplicity itself, as it is basically a flat plate. Matters may be complicated by the intrusion of the odd wheel, particularly in 4-4-0s and 4-6-0s. These are usually covered by a rectangular splasher-cum-seat, not a difficult item to fabricate. Once again, all this is basically a fitting job, and it may be useful to produce a simple paper template, which can be used as a guide for cutting out the metal parts. Even so, it is well to leave a mm or so on the waste side, to give a little bit of 'fat' for final fitting.

Where the cab floor incorporates splashers, or other raised sections of footplate, I build this all up as a unit on the bench, fitting it to the loco as a last operation. I usually just tack cab floors into place with 145°, rather than trying to run seam joints. Don't forget

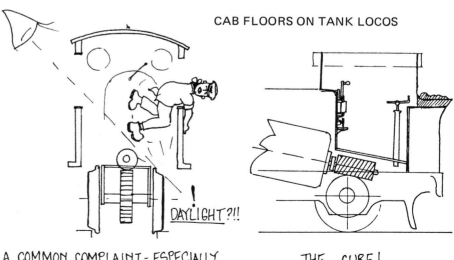

CAB FLOORS ON TANK LOCOS

A COMMON COMPLAINT - ESPECIALLY BAD IN OO GAUGE!   THE CURE!

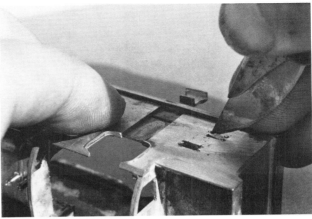

These bunker steps on the N7 are just the sort of detail variation that can call for some quite tricky work on a cast kit. The openings are pierced by drilling four holes in the corners, and joining up with a craft knife. The resulting holes are dressed to shape with a file. The actual steps are made up as a sub-assembly, to be fitted from the rear. The step is soldered to its backing with a higher-melt solder, which is also used to tin the rest of the strip so that the finished job can be soldered in place with 70° lowmelt. The finished result is worth the effort.

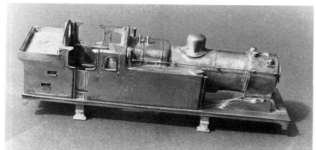

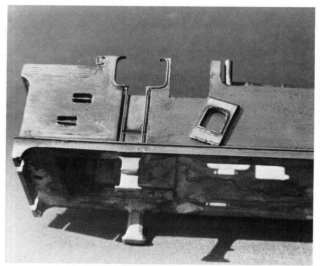

Major surgery on the 'N7'. The version I was modelling had a cab window located further aft than that catered for by the kit. The window and surrounding metal were cut out and re-located, and the resulting hole was filled with scrap whitemetal. A bit of filling and finishing made all good. The cuts were made with a razor saw (sides) and craft knife (bottom), allowing the maximum possible 'margin' around the window.

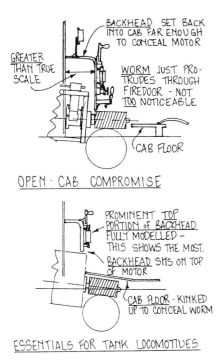

OPEN · CAB COMPROMISE

ESSENTIALS FOR TANK LOCOMOTIVES

BACKHEAD BODGES

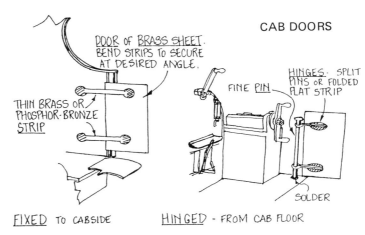

FIXED TO CABSIDE   HINGED - FROM CAB FLOOR

CAB DOORS

to ensure that you allow any necessary clearances for sideplay of the rear drivers where your cab floor incorporates splashers. And, of course, in 00 these will need to be arranged for the narrower-than-scale gauge, which may leave your footplatemen a bit short of elbow room.

Cab interiors are one area where I have found that Plastikard may successfully and readily be substituted for metal, in those locomotives where the structure of the kit does not need the benefit of the floor being soldered in place. Again, tank engines are more likely to be strong enough for a glued-in or even loose-fitted cab interior. 0-6-0 tender engines such as the Finecast 4F or 2251 can do with all the help they can get in holding the back end together!

Backheads are another component much ignored by the cast-kit makers, especially where the kit design puts a large chunk of magnet where the fire-door should be! I have found it well worth while to attempt some representation of the backhead even if it is not in full view. Where there are unavoidable mechanical intrusions, it may be necessary either to alter the position of the backhead in relation to the cab front, perhaps by moving it out into the cab by a few mm to clear the motor. Or, where the motor is low-mounted in the chassis, the backhead may lose its lower half, and sit on top of the magnet. The sketches give some alternatives.

The actual modelling of backheads I find a particularly satisfying exercise, although some whitemetal kits do provide truly excellent cab detail which cannot reasonably be bettered.

These are generally the more recent productions of the better manufacturers, so if the kit you are using for your model is older or cruder, then a little pleasant modelling is indicated. I usually work in metal, and find the etched handwheels and gauges available from George Norton invaluable. Plastikard, however, also lends itself to this sort of work, and I produce backheads in both materials. There are various cast and etched fittings available, and often the main problem is information. Access to preserved locos, the more detailed of drawings or, if you're lucky, photographs, will give a lead. A simple representation of the principal features is a lot better than nothing at all!

One last item that is often best incorporated with the cab floor of a tender engine is the fall-plate, a hinged metal flat that covers the gap twixt engine and tender. These were often

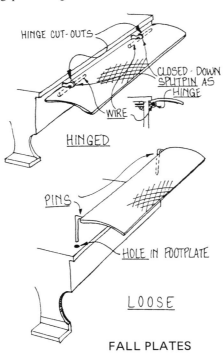

FALL PLATES

of non-slip chequer-plate steel, and etched chequer-plate can be obtained to enable this feature to be reproduced — a nice touch. It is best to either hinge the fall-plate, or make it as a separate component located by pins dropping into holes in the rear edge of the cab floor (Mike Sharman's method). Both are illustrated in the sketch.

Tank engines also need the bunker shovelling plate to complete the cab interior, and don't forget that the sidetanks often — but not always — extend back into the cab. Particularly true of 0-6-0s or 0-6-2Ts, where the bottom of the tank is the wheel splasher. Backheads are as tender engines, but the interior of the cab will be further cluttered by the handbrake standard and rear sandboxes, where these are not incorporated into the bunker. Prototype data required, as usual!

Cab doors are another item much ignored by the manufacturers of cast whitemetal kits, especially on tender engines. Again, these are simplicity itself to produce, although if you want to actually hinge them, life becomes a little trickier. It is obviously much simpler to fix them in one position, and I generally settle for closed on mainline passenger engines, and partly or wholly open on goods engines or shunters. If you have made the cab interior as a separate sub-assembly in metal, it is often possible to incorporate the cab doors in this, when they may indeed be hinged (see the sketch).

CAB ROOFS

The cab roof of a model locomotive is a lot more prominent than the full-sized equivalent, for obvious reasons. It amazes me how often kit manufacturers contrive to get this vital component wrong — and just what a difference putting matters right can make to the 'look' of the finished model. A classic case is the Finecast 'King', which totally lacks any of the prototype locomotive's prominent rivet detail. Also frequently noted for their absence are ventilators, overlap plates and rainstrips.

The manufacture of a new cab roof is a relatively straightforward and satisfying piece of

A brass cab roof for the 'N7', as well as looking better and allowing the correct roof variant to be modelled, also permitted an 'open' roof vent.

Scribe the line of the rivets on the inside of the cab roof (a pass with a dark-coloured permanent marker helps scribe-lines show up), and away you go. Riveting tools are self-spacing, otherwise I judge the effect by eye. I never attempt to get the full number of rivets on, unless they are very widely spaced — the result always looks overdone, as the rivets are inevitably overscale. I usually aim for about two-thirds the correct number, but tend to rely on my eye. If it looks right . . . If the metal you are using is very hard, it may not take rivet impressions from a scriber. Soften it a bit by heating — not too much, certainly nowhere near red-heat — and quenching to relieve the temper a bit. Relieves your temper as well!

With the rivets duly impressed, the rest of the relief detail can be added. The ventilator slide itself — a scrap of thin metal — plus the guides, from fine strip (fret waste again) are best sweated in place. Use plenty of flux, tin the joining faces well, more flux, and don't

metalwork. And what a difference the use of thin sheet metal makes, compared with a great chunky casting! Even if the loco has a roof devoid of all detail, it's still worthwhile substituting 10 thou brass or nickel-silver just to capture the correct 'look' of the edges.

Once again, this is basically a fitting job, so allow a bit of waste metal to work with. If the roof is complex in shape, as on a Gresley 'V2' or many LMS tender engines, a paper template may be derived from the cast floor of the kit (provided it is a reasonable fit) and used to rough out the metal. For a plain rectangular roof, I cut and trim to finished length, but leave myself quite a bit of excess width to play with, as it is very difficult to determine this dimension exactly until you've curved the metal. This is the vital process, for we need a very accurate fit to the cab front (and rear, if it has one). Once again, a bit of dowel, fingers, and constant offering-up to the cast cab structure will produce the desired result.

With the sheet-metal sitting down nicely on the cab structure, mark off the width required. You will probably find that the cast cab has gone well out of square, particularly on tender engines, where handling tends to pinch the rear of the cabsides together. Tweak this back straight (fingers!) before cutting the cab roof — any wonky angles here will stick out like a very sore thumb! In fact, even if you can't get the main cab structure absolutely 'true', still make the roof with accurate right-angles for the corners, as tapering overhangs are a lot less noticeable than trapezoidal roofs!

This will have produced a nice, square, well-fitting blank on which to base the cab-top detail. Before going any further, I tin the inside of the roof with 50/50 tinman's solder, to keep my joining options open. I also like to add a bit of interest — and a very prototypical touch — by modelling sliding cab-roof ventilators open or partly open. This, of course, entails making a hole in the roof at the appropriate

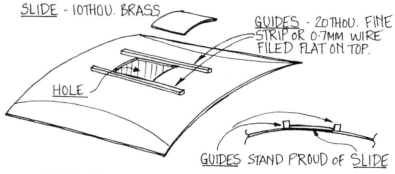

CAB ROOF VENTILATORS

location. A simple way to do this is to mark out and drill the biggest possible hole in the waste material to be removed from the cut-out. A small square Swiss file can be introduced through the drill-hole, and the aperture carefully filed out to size.

It is now time to add the relief detail. Rivets will need to be embossed, working from the back of the metal. (If you've got rivets to emboss, leave the tinning of the roof until after you've put them in, or the solder will dull the impressions.) Rivets can be embossed with a scriber, a small punch, or, best of all, a purpose-made modelmaker's riveting tool. The one that I use is made by Dick Ganderton, available from him direct (see suppliers appendix). Otherwise, I use a scriber, pressing firmly with the metal supported on a suitable surface — a piece of flat hardwood or an old vinyl floor tile are good, but best of all is lead sheet. Try your local builder for an offcut. Punches are not so good unless used with extreme discretion, although an old-fashioned gramophone needle (not too sharp) gripped in a pin vice is quite useful; hit it too hard, and the needle merely slides up in the vice rather than distorting or puncturing the job.

forget it's the solder that transfers the heat from bit to job. You can't sweat with a 'dry' iron.

Quite a lot of cab roofs — Deeley/Fowler LMS types, for instances — are built up of overlapping plates. These need representing by overlays onto the basic cab roof. In some instances, too, the overlays have rivet detail, or incorporate the ventilator. Which means more embossing, drilling and filing, but otherwise presents no additional difficulties. The overlays are best sweated in place, and if they are large, this should be completed before any attempt is made to add smaller detail. We all know the catch 22 syndrome, when bit A comes unsoldered when piece B is being soldered on, and when you try re-soldering bit A, then piece B comes adrift . . . . The answer is, firstly, to ensure that the joints that need the most heat are made first, and secondly, where the parts are roughly equal in mass, to apply a heatsink (bulldog clip, Dinky hair curler, paper clip or what-have-you) to the first joint while the second is made. A good vocabulary helps, too . . . .

Once the basic structure of the cab roof has been achieved, then the rainstrips and edge beadings may be added. These are just like any other beading, except for curved cab rainstrips. These I always make from wire rather than strip, as they need to be curved in two dimensions; the actual curve of the rainstrip, plus the need to lie flat on a curved surface, the cab roof. Only a circular-section material is happy being manipulated in this way, and it's easy enough to file the top, visible surface flat once all is safely soldered in place .... These curved rainstrips do need to be symmetrical, and I have found a scrap of ordinary graph paper a useful reference to check this.

The last job on the cab roof before it is finally fitted atop the cab is to clean up the metalwork. The sharpened screwdriver will chase out excess solder around beadings or rainstrips, while the three-sided scraper will take solder off the plain surface of the cab roof. If you should have the misfortune to get a blob of solder onto rivet detail, it can be removed by re-fluxing the area generally with phosphoric flux, melting the unwanted solder (preferably from behind — the underside of the roof is tinned, don't forget, so a touch of flux and an application of the iron with solder on the bit will ensure rapid heat transfer), and brushing it off with a fibreglass brush. Avoid the use of abrasives, which rob detail of crispness, and use the scrapers gently, to avoid digging-in and marking the surface.

Last job is to fit the roof to the cab. In the case of many tank engines, to which cab interior detail has been added, the fixing of the cab roof during assembly will make the painting of the cab detail and the addition of that desirable 'extra', the crew, somewhat tricky,

SPRING LUGS ON CAB ROOF

if not impossible. In these cases, I either glue the roof on once painting is complete, or adapt it to a push-fit by using spring lugs, as in the sketch.

On tender engines, I solder the roof in place, but tend only to tack it rather than flowing seams. This makes it easier to adjust, for it is vital that the cab roof be 'square' to the main structure of the locomotive; nothing looks worse than a cab roof whose edges are patently out of parallel with the footplate, and at some angle other than a right-angle to the boiler axis. Even if the cab isn't square, the roof must be.

A rivet-embossed brass smokebox wrapper being added to a 'pre-revision' Finecast 'J69'. The revised kit provides for this variation.

SMOKEBOX WRAPPERS

Mention has been made of the occasional desirability of adding a sheetmetal wrapper to the smokebox. There are a number of reasons for doing this; the kit may have a smokebox of insufficient diameter, or it may be smooth when it should have a bad attack of iron acne. Then, the rivets might be on the casting, but have been irretrievably damaged during preparation of the castings. Whatever the reason, the remedy is the same; some thin sheet metal must be arranged to conform to the radius of the smokebox, and firmly attached thereto.

A lot will depend on the actual way in which the loco goes together; is the smokebox fully circular, or is some part of the saddle cast integrally with it? Chances are, it'll be the latter, as this is more difficult to accommodate! The first job is to cut a strip of sheet the correct width for the smokebox, but plenty long enough to wrap around it. The metal wants to be thin, no more than 10 thou. The 8 thou brass used for many etched kits is fine, and even 5 thou shim can be used.

Rivets come next, if there are any. They are embossed exactly as described for the cab roof, although a lighter touch will be needed with the thin metal. If there are lines of horizontal rivets part-way up the smokebox or on the saddle, establish their position by wrapping a strip of paper over the smokebox, and marking in pencil. While you're at it, locate the top centreline, the hole for the chimney and the lower extremities of the smokebox or saddle. These salient points can be transferred to the metal wrapper, and any necessary holes drilled.

Once the wrapper is prepared, the strip is cut more-or-less to length (paper strip again), allowing a 'handling' excess at each end of at least 5 mm. The overlay is now annealed, to make it malleable enough to fit snugly around the contours of the smokebox. Heat it — not too much — in a gas flame, and quench it in cold water. It will be dull purple, and the rear face will need cleaning with fine wet-

and-dry before it will take solder. Take great care, as the wrapper will now be very soft and will mark easily; it needs the support of the cast smokebox before it'll take much handling.

Now comes the tricky bit — fixing it in place. Tin the inside of the wrapper thinly with 50/50 tinman's solder, then using the chimney-hole as a datum, carefully press the soft metal to shape over the cast smokebox. Once it's sitting snugly, with the vital front edge aligned, it can be soldered in place. Flood the whole issue with flux, and introduce a generous blob of 70° alloy through the chimney-hole whilst holding the wrapper firmly in contact with the smokebox. Ouch! But never mind. Repeat the process at the lower edges, keeping the wrapper as tight as you can. If you've been sufficiently generous with the solder and, especially, the flux, you'll find the wrapper will be fixed firmly for a fair proportion of the circumference.

If you feel that it needs a bit more, re-flux (it gets drawn in by capillary action) and reheat by applying the iron to the extremity or chimney hole; let the heat flow through the solder. It is possible, by repeating this process, and by periodically introducing a bit more solder, to sweat the entire wrapper into place. But it's rarely necessary — don't forget that the handrail stanchions and the plumbing will all help retain it.

All that now remains is to trim off the excess metal at the lower edges, and to file it all square and tidy. And if it all goes agley, don't despair — remember that the 70° alloy can all be melted out by dunking the issue in boiling water. But if you proceed carefully, and don't try and complete the soldering until you've established the alignment, all should be well. If you're worried about getting the front edge of the wrapper correctly aligned with the smokebox, try making it a mite too wide to give some excess at this edge, which can be filed back once the heat's died down. The oper-

Roy Jackson's beautifully natural K1, built from the Nu-cast kit. This is a 'Dunwich' regular and demonstrates the attraction of 'workhorse' engines. A mixed traffic 2–6–0 like this is ideal motive power for almost any post-grouping steam era layout.

ation is well worthwhile, and there are even etched wrappers commercially available for some cast locos, such as Gem's LNWR 2–4–0 and 2–4–2Ts (Brassmasters).

BOILER FITTINGS

The major boiler fittings of a locomotive, particularly the chimney, are major determinants of the engine's character and appearance. For any model to successfully capture that character, then the boiler fittings must look right. Notice that I say 'look right'. I have come across any number of instances where the boiler fittings of a model looked wrong, yet in terms of dimensional accuracy could not be faulted. The problem usually turned out to be rims and other relief detail at dead scale size failing to throw sufficient shadow to 'read' as strongly as they did on the prototype; or maybe the dead-scale diameter, with the different view points, lighting and general 'mass' of the model as against the real thing resulted in a 'too thick' or 'too thin' look. At all events it has been my experience that visual adjustments have to be made, and often this means departing from dead scale.

On the other hand, many cast-kit boiler fittings suffer from expediency. Thick rims and bases are easier to cast, even if they look clumsy. Chimneys and safety valve bonnets, through which excess kettle-effluent is wont to pass on real engines, are frequently chocked solid with metal. And, of course, there is the matter of the copper-cap and the brassy dome, never really convincing when rendered in paint.

So, all-in-all, there is a strong case for seeing if something a cut above the kit offering be contrived or purchased, although it must be said that some cast-kit boiler fittings are truly excellent, and almost impossible to better.

Fortunately, the model trade is strong on boiler fittings, with several substantial ranges to choose from, although, even so, it is still impossible to find a truly convincing chimney for quite a lot of locomotives. The Springside range of GWR copper-tops are lovely, though, and with their removable rims are easy to paint. Springside also have good brass domes, cleverly contrived and replete even to the bolt-bespattered innards! Pricey, but worth it. There are some good lost-wax items in the Cotswold and Slaters ranges, not to mention those made by that fellow Rice. Turned chimneys are available from specialists like George Norton, or Kemp Models. Once again, there are good, bad and indifferent, so critical choosing is the only answer.

However, it is by no means imperative to abandon the cast chimney or what-have-you from the kit. A bit of careful work can often bring vast improvements. The first job is to bore the chimney out, if it's one of the all-too-prevalent solid specimens. Where the chimney is fairly tall, there's no need to go right through, just so long as the eye 'reads' the chimney as hollow. Start by carefully drilling a smallish hole (about 1 mm/No.50) as near as you can get it to the centre of the chimney-top. A lot of cast chimneys are not quite circular — an aside of the mould-making process — so I judge it as best I can by eye. It is also essential to get this pilot hole as near vertical as possible. Failing a vertical drill, get down so that you can sight the drill as you work it (pin-vice and fingers, please — no electric short-cuts), and keep moving your viewpoint through a 90° arc to check the drill is not attempting to come out of the side of the chimney. Even if you do have a pillar drill of some sort, I still find it pays to take off the drive belt and twiddle the chuck by hand — it gives a far greater degree of control for this delicate operation.

Once there is a pilot hole down the chimney barrel, it is simply a matter of opening this out with successively larger drills until a bore of suitable diameter has been achieved. Where the chimney is a bit oval, it pays to drill slightly undersize, and to finalise the hole with a coarse round rat-tailed Swiss file; better that the top of the rim should appear of constant thickness than the bore be truly circular. The same applies for tapering chimneys, where the top is of greater diameter than the base. Drill to the largest practicable size, then finish off with the file, or, if you have it, with a suitable taper reamer or brooch. Much the same procedure is adopted with respect to safety valve bonnets, where these are not being replaced by brass — and don't forget that since the grouping, much brass was painted over. The post-1923 GW tank with burnished brass bonnet is one of the classic modelling clichés — but usually inaccurate for all that.

The other great failing of many cast chimneys and valve bonnets is the clumsiness imparted by over-thick edges. To cast truly fine rims and skirts to a chimney requires high-class mould-making and very careful production, if the castings are to emerge fully-formed, clean and consistent. Many manufacturers opt for the easier option of beefing-up the patterns — it makes for cheaper, simpler mouldings at the cost of a rather dismal result in model-making terms. All is not lost, however. Provided that the chimney or whatever is otherwise of good quality and reasonable accuracy, then it is well worth going to town at the preparation stage, and carefully thinning down the obtrusive edges. Round and oval Swiss files, the scraper and a cocktail stick covered with 400 grit wet-and-dry will work wonders around the lip of the chimney rim, and over the edges of the skirt where it meets the smokebox.

It is important to bear in mind the way that the eye 'reads' the model, so that we attend to the points that give us our appreciation of the shape of the component. Basically, we see reflections and shadows as our strongest visual references. Edges such as a chimney rim stand out as highlights, and it is this which reinforces our impression of their thickness. It is the same effect that enables us to give the illusion that a cast cabside a scale 3 inches thick is actually of thin sheet, merely by tapering the visible edges; those are what the eye 'reads'. The other essentials are to ensure that the chimney rim has sufficient overhang to throw the right amount of shadow, and that the curves at cap and base also 'read' right. Photographs are the invaluable aid, while using the silhouette of the chimney against a sheet of white paper will help the eye to judge curvatures exactly.

Whilst we are chivvying the chimney and the other boiler fittings about, it is as well to ensure that they have the right base radius to sit properly on boiler or smokebox. This is another favourite cast-kit failing, resulting in the chimney or dome that perches atop the boiler with the edges of the skirt flapping in the breeze. Provided that there is a sufficiency of metal to work with (this is where over-thick skirts to cast fittings can be a life-saver, so check the fit before you thin them down), the fit may be vastly improved by wrapping the boiler or smokebox (or a piece of dowel of equivalent diameter) with some fairly coarse wet-and-dry (120 grit) and gently rubbing the offending fitting to and fro to remove unwanted metal. Once it is sitting snugly atop the boiler,

Mounting boiler fittings. The use of epoxy allows time for adjustment, while the square provides a reference to help get them all upright.

SEATING DOWN BOILER FITTINGS

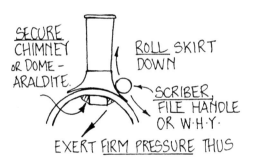

then the skirt can be finish-dressed from above with the files and so on to get the thin edge that convinces. It is also possible to 'roll' a skirt down onto a boiler using a screwdriver or piece of bar.

If the boiler-mountings have spigots to locate them into holes in the boiler, do check that these position the fittings in the vertical mode. Frequently, an accumulation of patternmaking, casting and assembly errors can result in the chimney leaning rakishly to the left while the dome makes a bob to the right, with the safety valve at some point between! The usual remedy is to open out the holes a trifle, so that the fittings may be accurately aligned, both with respect to each other and to the vertical axis of the boiler. Use the small engineers' square or mount the boiler on the footplate and sight against the cabsides.

Where the prototype has a splendid brass dome, and the kit provides no more than a doughy leaden affair, then there is no real option but to substitute brass for lead. I'm never convinced that lost-wax cast brass domes will ever look as good as the real McCoy, turned and polished. But they are certainly a good deal more convincing than mere painted

whitemetal, and it is worth taking some trouble to get a good surface. The first thing is to choose a good casting, one free of excessive flash, prominent part-lines and with a good, smooth surface. The refining process comes next, although one would not expect a lost-wax dome to need much work in this respect. Then, it's all down to elbow-grease, unless you know an obliging jeweller with a polishing mop. Fine (600 grit) wet-and-dry to polish off the mould-marks, then a fibreglass burnisher, followed by an old toothbrush and Brasso. And more toothbrush, and more Brasso. And so on, and so on, until the surface starts to take on the smooth, hard gloss of real polish, when I go over to Duraglit and a soft duster for the final bulling-up.

I always either force, screw or glue-fit brass domes, so that they can be kept clear of the painting process, and also so that they can be removed from time-to-time for re-polishing when in service. Turned domes are easier to polish, and if you turn them yourself, it is easy to arrange the screw-mounting. But those are operations that lie outside the scope of this particular opus.

The smaller cast boiler fittings, such as Ross pop safety valves, whistles and snifting valves, are usually in worse case than their bigger brethren, being almost impossible to clean up and often badly ovalled. Replacement by small turnings, either trade or home-made, is the best answer. Quite a good Gresley snifting valve can, however, be contrived from a 10 or 12BA cheesehead screw with a blob of solder run into the slot of the head. Small cheesehead screws can also substitute for sandbox fillers and boiler plugs.

Other boiler fittings worth looking at are the smokebox door darts, often rather crude, the washout plugs and the lifting eyes, if present. There are some delightful turned brass smokebox darts from the Far East widely available which are better than anything the kit-maker is likely to provide. Darts and washout plugs are available as lost-wax castings. Where washout plugs are recessed, they can be produced by drilling a hole to suit the recess, blanking off behind with some thin metal, and drilling for wire plugs, much as was done to reinstate rivets. Lifting eyes can be neatly represented with a tiny loop of 5 amp fusewire set into a hole.

OTHER DETAILS

Other details often absent or poorly produced on whitemetal kits are lubricators and reversing reach-rods. Cast lubricators are often little more than misshapen approximations. A lot can be done to make them more convincing by adding the various feed-pipes and a decent handwheel (this comes etched on George Norton's cab fittings fret). The fitting of the pipework was illustrated in the 'plumbing' section of the last chapter. Or there are better milled-brass and lost-wax alternatives which may be substituted.

Reversing rods are a vital part of the valve-gear, and the first thing to check is that they link up, at least visually, with the rest of the gear. Do they enter the cab in the right place to meet up with the reverser? And do they reach the cross-shaft or the lifting links at the fore end? Cast reach-rods are often too thick and clumsy, and are also very fragile and prone to handling damage. I like to make mine from thin nickel-silver sheet or strip, adding bracket detail from fret waste and pivot-pins from wire, as shown in the sketch. The better kits these days tend to have parts like these as etchings, a vast improvement. Reversing reach-rods were also among the last parts of the steam engine to be painted over, and even in the late BR period, burnished reach-rods were not unknown, even if the rest of the loco was a depressing study in grime.

To return for a moment to our two contrasting examples held up at the beginning of this chapter, we will now have done much to bring our cast-whitemetal locomotive up to the standard set by the faceless Hong Kong minions who produce Mainline's masterpiece. Much of what is left to be done is beneath the footplate. But there are still a number of other

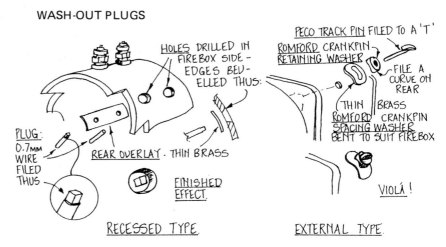

WASH-OUT PLUGS

RECESSED TYPE.

EXTERNAL TYPE.

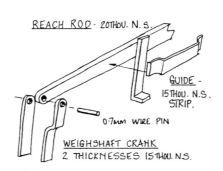

REVERSING ROD

improvements and refinements we can essay in our quest for an individual and accurate model.

Although less obvious when the loco is 'in service', I like to make some attempt to model the drag beams of both loco and tender, to at least resemble the prototype. This is sheet-metal work akin to the cab roof, and in practical terms is no more difficult. Compromise may be needed to accommodate the loco-to-tender coupling, but something a good deal less obtrusive than the truly massive hooks so often provided by kit-makers is easily contrived.

One engineering point to consider is that, ideally, the loco should take the 'pull' of tender and train at as close to the driving-axle centre-height as possible. This often entails putting the drawgear in the middle of the drag-beams — which is, after all, where the prototype puts it, hence the name! Whilst in this part of the engine's anatomy, another nice touch is to model the water-hoses that feed from the tender to the injectors — see the drag-beam illustrations for a way of doing this. It adds a lot to the loco when viewed in silhouette.

The tender, too, will benefit from some detail improvements and a few additions. Cast brake and scoop standards often leave much to be desired, and may be replaced by trade items, or by home-made renderings of tube, handrail knobs and wire, as illustrated in the sketch. Fillers can acquire hinges, grab-irons or handles, clamps and latches. Toolboxes often lack hinges, hasps, padlocks. All can be added from scraps of strip, wire and shim, even Plastikard and cyano. Tender vents are available as turnings if the cast ones are no good, and a set of fire-irons from fine pin-wire and shim are a delightful finishing touch. No steam loco went far without them .... Underneath, as well as the brake-hangers and rigging, there was usually (but not always) a water-scoop, available as castings from several sources if

The importance of the silhouette. The feed-hole between loco and tender on Alan Ketley's '9F' are one of those little touches that 'lift' the model into a truly convincing miniature.

Here is my 'J39/2' at the unpainted stage. A nickel-silver reverser reach-rod has been added, while the offside of the loco has acquired fuse-wire lubricator pipes and a lost-wax cast lubricator, complete with drive linkage.

Vive la différence! On the right, the K3 smokebox door supplied in the kit. On the left, an improved version of the same casting, with brass strip hinges on a brass wire pivot bar, lost-wax cast smokebox dart, and fitted with its handrail and lamp-iron — much easier to do this before the door is installed on the loco.

place. All this I do with tinman's solder, so that nothing comes adrift when I sweat the overlays in place with 70° alloy. I never bother to spring the front screw coupling, and often solder the hook to the overlay, which enables me to poke the tail of the hook through the cast bufferbeam, and use it to tack the whole overlay assembly in place, prior to the final joining. Once all the soldering is accomplished, it will often be necessary to open out the holes in the buffer-housings to allow the shanks of the buffer-heads to pass through.

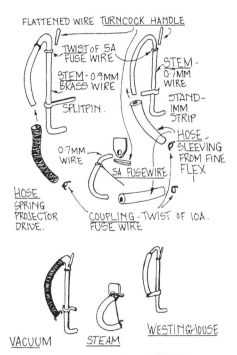

BUFFER-BEAM HOSES

I usually make my own brake and steam-heat hoses. W & T do some fine-wound spring drive cable which makes lovely vacuum hose, or guitar strings are good. I base the standards on wires of suitable diameter, and add stop-cocks and bracket detail with fine wire. Westinghouse connections, being pressure rather than vacuum hose, lack the wire-wound re-inforcement, and are best represented by plain wire. They are also a lot smaller in diameter than vacuum hose. Steam-heat and air-operated push-pull hoses are pressure hoses, too, though steam-heat pipes do often have the wire-reinforcement. The sketches and photos will show the methods and the results. Again, this is one of those aspects of the model where a bit of attention and trouble pay handsome dividends.

I could go on pointing up specific examples of how the kit-based model may be improved in all manner of subtle ways for another twenty pages, but by now the principles will be apparent. What you will need to do depends upon your own inclination, the quality of the kit, and the prototype.

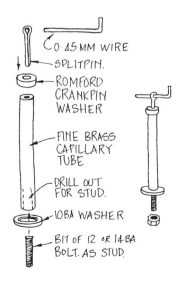

BRAKE STANDARDS

your kit is lacking. The rear coal-plate might look better in thin sheet, too. . . .

A last weak area worth some detailed attention is the buffer-beams. Many kits are devoid of detail in this area, and cast buffers are universally horrid. Most people like to substitute the turned, sprung variety. Those from Kean-Maygib and Allan Gibson are particularly easy to fit, and the heads and springs are always better installed once the loco has been painted. But what of those bare beams, where the prototype has rivets and bolts galore? Thin sheet overlays are the answer, with the rivet-detail duly embossed, as described for cab-roof and smokebox wrapper. I saw off cast buffers and file the faces of the buffer-beams back a bit with my big mill bastard file. A hole (or pair of linked holes to form a slot) of suitable size to clear the drawbar of the front coupling hook is now drilled on the centreline, plus holes to accept pipework if required, and, of course, the clearance holes for the sprung buffers.

The overlays are prepared, the reverse being tinned, and the buffer-housings soldered in

One of the advantages of whitemetal locos is that they provide a relatively painless way of producing an adequate selection of motive power for a large layout, at a reasonable cost in time and money. Geoff Kent's L1, built for 'Dunwich' from a 10-year-old East Coast Joint Models kit (now available from ABS), is a good example of a 'layout' loco.

CHAPTER SEVEN

FINISHING—PREPARATION AND BASIC PAINTING

Before becoming embroiled in the minutiae of finishing and painting our whitemetal locomotive, a word of caution. There is a tendency, I've found, for the final stages of the completion and painting of a model locomotive to acquire an accelerative will of their own. After weeks, maybe months of steady, thoughtful, nay, contemplative modelling, suddenly there is light at the end of the tunnel. The temptation is to rush, perchance to skimp, probably to omit, and almost certainly to compromise. Hold hard! It is time for more appraisal. We do not want to defeat our careful preparation, meticulous assembly and painstaking detailing by over-eager applications of paint to an ill-prepared surface These words are written by one who has done so, and more than once!

THE SUB-ASSEMBLY SYNDROME

Mention has been made at various points in this diatribe to the notion of producing our locomotive superstructure in a number of sub-assemblies, arranged with the final painting in mind. The kit instructions, of course, make no mention of any such proceeding — but then, as they rarely take any cognisance of the likelihood of the finished model being painted, this is scarcely surprising! However, it is usually not too difficult to arrange, and is very well

worth doing, even if the final livery of the locomotive in question is unlined black (and there's more to that one than you might suppose). The photographs illustrate a couple of examples, the 'H' class tank in full SECR livery at one extreme, and the 'J39' in plain BR black at the other.

These two examples serve to show the basic divisions which aid matters. The 'H' is arranged so that the boiler, smokebox, firebox and the tops of the sidetanks form one unit, and the rest of the loco minus the cab roof another, whilst the cab roof, sandboxes, steps and one or two other details were left off until painting was complete. This is, of course, just about the most complex and elaborate of the pre-grouping liveries, and it would not be

necessary to go to quite these lengths had the loco been finished in SR lined olive or BR black. The 'J39', whilst a very much simpler painting proposition, was a much trickier modelling job, as it has had a boiler fillet spliced in, a front made to the firebox, a lot of cast detail (inappropriate to this version) removed, and finer boiler-bands fitted during painting. However, having the boiler as a separate assembly during painting helped to ensure that the paint could be airbrushed evenly over the whole model, without either getting too much on prominent areas or leaving 'shaded' areas thin.

So how were these sub-divisions of the models arranged? In the case of the 'H', very simply. The design of the kit was such that

My 'J39/2', No. 64899, in BR plain black — all five shades of it! This is a much modified Finecast kit, which has now received further detailing and weathering.

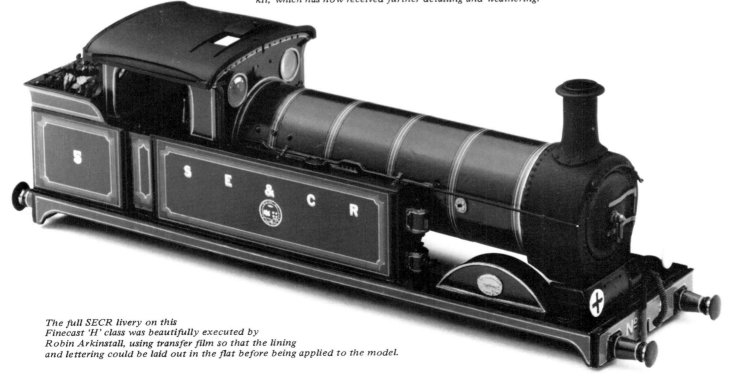

The full SECR livery on this Finecast 'H' class was beautifully executed by Robin Arkinstall, using transfer film so that the lining and lettering could be laid out in the flat before being applied to the model.

all that had to be done was merely not to join these two units together. Such is the quality of the kit and the fit of the parts that the boiler was a good push-fit onto the rest of the loco-motive, so all that was need once painting was complete was a touch of adhesive — UHU in this case — to keep things together. On the 'J39', matters were a good deal more complex. This model was built from the original Wills 'J39' kit, a bit of an outdated horror (the model was in fact built as a 'study' for the new version of the kit). This entailed a new footplate en-tirely, and the opportunity was naturally taken to model the smokebox saddle correctly, which, in turn, meant dispensing with those parts of the saddle originally cast integrally with the boiler — the great big file job! The boiler assembly locates into the cab-front at the firebox end (the backhead detail is actually modelled as part of the boiler), while at the front it is held by a self-tapping screw from beneath the smokebox saddle, up into the bot-tom of the smokebox casting. Self-tapping screws work very well in whitemetal, so long as they are not removed frequently. As, once the loco is painted, there is no need for further disassembly, they are ideal for holding cast body sub-assemblies together, and are very simple to use.

Really, it is the boiler that is the bugbear; if you can remove that from the rest of the model, then all manner of constructional and painting problems can be overcome. There are, however, certain other bits that it pays to make removable. Cab roofs on tank engines we have mentioned, but smoke deflectors can cause major problems, while fittings, such as West-inghouse pumps that may need painting and lining on their own account, are best left off until this has been carried out. Similarly, other fittings that obstruct the painting process can be kept out of the way. Ever tried lining behind the springs on a Kirtley tender, or those on a GW outside-frame 4-4-0 that come right in front of the splashers? Not easy ... If you are faced with a truly elaborate livery, then it may pay to leave quite a lot of bits off until all those subtle stripes and whorls are executed. Toolboxes and sandboxes, clacks, feed-pumps and so on are readily fitted with adhesive once the paint is hard, and I've never found any problems attaching small bits in this way. The last category of 'removable for painting' items are those which essentially don't want paint-ing. Shiny brass domes and safety valves, sprung buffer-heads and, of course, any glaz-ing are all better off out of the way. Small polished metal fittings, however, such as pipes or handrails, are best firmly secured to the model (unless they obstruct the lining), and either masked off or scraped clear of paint at the end of the job.

PREPARATION
Having carefully appraised our model to ensure that we have got it broken down into the most suitable form for painting, it is now

time to take a good look at the state of the surface, to see if this is in a fit state to take the finish. Obviously, the metal must be as clean as we can get it, but the first job is to check carefully for any unremoved traces of misplaced solder, any solder-filled angles with tell-tale meniscus curves, and a last check to make sure things like splashers, toolboxes and cab roofs are truly square to the footplate. Once the model is painted, colour differentiation between, say, a splasher and a footplate, will mercilessly announce any departure from the parallel!

Once you are truly satisfied that all is as square and well-dressed as possible — and this is where the temptation to skimp and hurry must be resisted if the result is not to be com-promised — then the painting process can start. The first thing that I do is a little unconven-tional, but I find it a great help to paint adhe-sion; I dose the whole model with a liberal coat of phosphoric acid, applied with a small paintbrush, and leave it to stand for an hour or two. With luck, the whole model will go a dull, patchy grey. This may not look as nice as the 'bull-it-up-with-Brasso' approach, but it is a very sound basis for paint — as remarked earlier, it is in effect a 'phosphate dip' and hence a pretty good primer.

To clean up the model, I use a soft-to-medium toothbrush and 'Jif' or 'Ajax' scouring cream. First, I rinse the model off thoroughly in warm water to get rid of any excess acid from the surface. Then I squirt on a good dol-lop of the cream, and set to with my toothbrush to gently scrub the surface free of grease, flux and filings. Bear in mind where the fine detail, such as lamp-irons and lubricators, is located, and go easy at these points. There are places, of course, where the toothbrush will not reach, and for these I use a small hogshair paintbrush to scrub out the residues. Once the white foam has turned a nice grimy grey, I rinse the loco off under the tap — and start again. I repeat the process of gentle — and I mean gentle — scrubbing with scouring cream until the foam no longer discolours to any extent. Then I give the model a very thorough rinsing under a run-ning tap, and leave it to dry.

A few cautionary notes about cleaning. Firstly, steer very clear of those washing-up liquids and similar that promise to keep your hands as soft as your face (not much of a promise, in my case), as these contain lanolin, which will form an oily film over the surface of the model, just what we're trying to avoid. What is good for hands is not necessarily good for model railway locomotives — and vice-versa, in the case of the phosphoric acid! The scouring cream, by the by, is quite strongly alkaline, and will effectively neutralise any 'free' acid left on the model. Once the model is washed, it must be treated with real kid gloves. Don't handle it directly — interpose a tissue or clean lint-free cloth. Don't let it get dirty again — paint it as soon as practicable after cleaning, and keep it out of dirty or dusty

places. Whilst it is drying, keep it warm, but cover it — I have a metal loaf tin with a few ¼ in holes drilled around just under the rim, which I invert over the model, which stands on an ordinary shallow baking tray. This set-up is easy to keep clean and dust-free, and can be parked on a nightstore or the back of the Aga without problem. It also has writ large upon it: 'Painted model drying', after a dom-estic disaster some years since. . . .

I have heard of solvent-based cleaning pro-cesses, which can give almost clinically clean results — if you can get hold of the appropriate solvent. One is called 'Arklone', and is made by ICI, but is really an industrial process cleaner and tends to come in 50-gallon drums — which would clean an awful lot of models! There are also various ultrasonic cleaning sys-tems, widely used by US modellers, but again availability is the problem over here. Having said all that, Lofty Adcocks, who used to do all those superb paint jobs for K's, W & H and even Beeson back in the 1960s, merely sloshed a load of cellulose thinners over models before spraying them with neat cellu-lose (no primer) from an ordinary motor-trade spraygun! But he was a minor genius at such things — marvel at his wonderful models of early aircraft in the Science Museum if you want to see the stamp of the man.

PRIMING
There are all manner of 'camps' over the paint-ing of locomotives, and nowhere is this more true than in the desirability, or otherwise, of priming models. As I've already given mine a phosphate dip, I reckon this to be sufficient priming from the point of view of ensuring adhesion of the paint. So why, then, do I use a cellulose car primer? Mainly to 'fill' the sur-face, and also to give an even undercolour base to the livery. The type of grey primer sold in aerosol cans at your local motoring D-I-Y emporium is actually what is known in the car-body trade as a 'surfacing primer'. That is, it will fill any minute surface marks or inden-tations in the metal, and give a perfectly smooth basis for the finishing coats. I find it valuable in the same role on models, particu-larly on areas where the quality of the finish is particularly noticeable — boilers, tank sides, tender sides.

Some people go through an elaborate ritual of decanting this primer into an airbrush for spraying onto the model. I find that a well-shaken aerosol can is just as good. The object is to get a thin, but even, coat over the whole model. The section on 'spraying' gives a few pointers as to how this is best achieved, but there is no substitute for practice and a little experiment. I always spray primer onto a slightly warm model, which cuts the drying time down to seconds. But the real secret is to thoroughly shake the tin before cutting loose. Give it to the wife while she's doing her aerobics exercises — or you'll have to do some yourself. If the paint in the tin feels thick when you shake it — the old ball-bearing doesn't really want to move — then try immersing the can in hot water to warm the contents a bit. But don't put it on the stove to boil!

Once the model is coated with a nice, thin, even coat of the primer, it is time for yet another appraisal. One of the advantages of the light grey primer is that it is merciless at showing up faults. Rough bits of surface, unremoved solder, porosity, cracks, hollows and bumps all stand out, particularly if you examine the model in a strong directional light. Now is the time for some finish-filling and rubbing down.

Finish-filling was noted as part of the painting process, which it truly is. The material used is knife stopping, which is exactly the same thing as surfacing primer but a lot thicker, being in paste rather than liquid form. As these products are all based on cellulose thinners, it is easy to arrive at just the right consistency for the job in hand by 'letting-down' the stopping with a few drops of thinner — a small dropper from the chemist is a valuable tool for work like this. The knife stopping is applied with some thin, springy material, such as thin card or even Plastikard. Beware, though, as the stopping attacks this last and it can suddenly go all soft and gooey on you! Best of all is thin sheet polythene, which can be cut from the lid of an ice-cream container or out of an old polybottle such as the milk now comes in at Sainsburys.

Knife stopping is just the job for filling cracks, hollows, deep scratches or toolmarks, slight imperfections of fit and the almost inevitable surface porosity of some castings. Wipe it on, using the card or whatever as a leveller, and whip the surplus away at the end of each pass. It is amazing just how good a surface you can get over porous or gappy castings with this material, and as it is a cellulose, it will 'bite' the primer you've already applied, and stick into even the tiniest hollow or crack. Keep the stopping at the right consistency with the dropper of thinners — you will find by experiment what the job requires. I generally have mine at about the clotted cream stage, which ensures that it won't 'drag'. Once you've wiped the stopping on to all the required areas, let it dry thoroughly, and resist at all costs any temptation to go back over it before it has gone hard.

Having attended to the dips, it is now time to eradicate any unwanted bumps (which include excess stopping). A spot of rubbing-down is indicated. This is a notion regarded with horror in some quarters, but these cellulose primers are designed to be rubbed down, and it's worth taking the trouble. Once again, it is essential to support our abrasive with a reference backing, and I find that Mike Doherty's idea of sticking a sheet of very fine (400 grit or below) wet-and-dry paper to a sheet of $\frac{1}{16}$in balsa with Evo-stik and cutting off tiny rubbing-sticks makes the process a lot easier. Rubbing-down of paint should always be done 'wet', to keep the paper from clogging, so keep a little pot of clean water handy, and keep washing the rubbing-stick off. Surface residue can be wiped away with a damp tissue, and the model dried as before. Rubbing-down, as with so many other aspects of the kit-building process, cannot be hurried. Only the gentlest of pressures can be applied, and it may require several applications of primer followed by more gentle rubbing before the bigger bumps are eliminated, for you'll almost certainly end up with bare metal at least once during the proceedings.

It goes without saying that whilst all this filling and rubbing down is in progress, the model must be handled with care, and every effort must be made to keep grease and dirt off the surface — although there is no law against giving it another bath if handling becomes unavoidable. However, if we've done our basic assembly, filling, finishing and preparation with due care and attention, there shouldn't be a lot to do at this late stage of the game. What we are dealing with is minor blemishes, not fundamental faults. If you find handling with tissues cumbersome, it is poss-

The Stanier Black Fives were not as plain as many people think, as this view of Rod Neep's model of 45038 clearly shows. This is an example of a good kit 'lifted' to the highest level by skilful detailing and painting. This DJH kit is an example of the trend toward 'composite' kits, where thin sheet components such as cab sides are made as etchings rather than being cast.

ible to buy packs of disposable ultra-thin surgical gloves at some chemists or veterinary and farmers' suppliers. These are a cheap and simple way of keeping fingermarks off of models at this delicate stage of the proceedings, and they do not impair one's sense of touch as do domestic gloves.

Once the surface blemishes have been appropriately dealt with, I like to give the model another light coat of primer. This serves both to show whether the aforementioned blemishes have been efficiently eradicated, and also to give a nice even undercolour on which to apply the livery, which is where the fun truly starts.

WHAT COLOUR, WHAT PAINT?

Before going into the merits of the various paint formulations that are available, it is well to pause a moment and consider the matter of colour. Just what is Midland Red or Caley Blue (to name two of the real troublemakers) and how can they be represented? And why is it that some models look a lot more convincing in their colouring than others, which may be superficially more correct? A short fable is perhaps in order.

Many years ago, K's brought out a whitemetal 'bodyline' kit intended to fit the then-new Hornby-Dublo 2-rail 0–6–0T chassis. The prototype was the standard Johnson Midland Railway 0–6–0T, and the sample model was meticulously finished in fully-lined Midland livery. I was shown this model at the old Central Hall Easter show, and asked what I thought of the paint job. I remember expressing the opinion that I thought that the finish was superbly executed, but wasn't it a pity that it was the wrong colour. 'Whad'ye mean?' thundered Pop Keyser, 'Let me tell you, boy, that this is the real McCoy. It's genuine Midland crimson lake, mixed to their own formula.'

The point of this is that what might be right on the prototype isn't necessarily right on the model. Looking at a model, particularly a small-scale model (below 7 mm/ft) is equivalent to viewing the prototype at some considerable distance, which means that we would have some tens, if not hundreds, of metres of interposing atmosphere, which is by no means as transparent as a lot of people think it is! We are all familiar with the dim and misty horizon, but the effect is present over quite short distances. I will remember trying to pick out the right colour touch-up paint for my car by comparing the colour of the cap with that of the car, at the trifling separation of the width of an Exeter side-street. I was at least two shades out when I got close to . . . It is also a truism of colourwork that a small area of colour will always look darker than a large area of the same colour, due to the much smaller amount of light reflected, and the comparative lack of highlights. So it is not surprising that Ken Keyser's meticulous Midland Red should have looked more like plum purple to me.

Another factor of finish that is affected by the atmospheric dilution of perception is the matter of gloss. We are all familiar with the motor-car that looks nice and shiny from a distance, but looks dull, blotchy and smeary at close quarters. Distance tends to dull our appreciation of shine and highlight, but the mind automatically compensates. In painting our model, therefore, we need to compensate the other way, by dulling the finish of our model so that our eyes read it as a gleaming locomotive at a distance. An over-glossy finish (or its opposite, a dead matt one) tends to make the locomotive or whatever 'stand out' of the scene and look unnatural. This type of finish really only suits showcase models, designed to be viewed close-to and not in the context of a layout. And not many showcase models are built out of whitemetal kits. . . .

So ideally, we need to take the 'sting' out of both the colour and the gloss of our finishes so that our models will look right at the distances and under the conditions that we are normally accustomed to view them. There are two ways of doing this, either by modifying the paints themselves, or by using tinted varnishes of appropriate gloss. I always use the latter method, as it ensures that the same degree

A nice, restrained version of the Southern olive green livery, executed by John Newton on this Wealden Models ex-LBSC 'E4'. Alan Ketley built the model.

of dilution is applied to all the colours in the livery (and the lining, lettering and plates), and it facilitates the use of an intermediate high-gloss stage for lining, lettering and the application of transfers. It is also a lot easier than monkeying around trying to get 'corrected' colours, while, if skilfully applied, tinted varnish is both subtle and progressive, and allows several bites of the cherry.

Having disposed of the colour and degree of finish of our paint, there still remains the chemical aspect. Are we to use cellulose, oil or synthetic-based paints? Here, too, there are a number of factors to be considered — the finish required, the area to be covered, the means of application and the availability of the desired colour. I have always preferred cellulose paints for their superior adhesion, quick-drying and the hardness of the finish. There are also huge ranges of colours to choose from, and one-off colours are easily mixed to order, though you'll have to buy a litre or two! But even sticking to the car touch-up ranges like 'Brushing Belco', there are literally hundreds of shades to consider, and, remembering that we shall be 'killing' the colour with our tinted varnish, mere academic 'correctness' (almost impossible to assess anyway) is of less importance than a visually satisfying result.

The trade enamels such as Humbrol, DBI, Cherry and the synthetic ranges by Floquil and

Testors, can all be readily adjusted for spraying, and are probably easier if brush-painting is contemplated. If you are thinking of brush-painting a large loco, though, avoid the quicker-drying paints, or you could have problems with brushing-out. Humbrol or, for smaller areas, the xylene-based synthetics are OK, but I must say I do prefer to spray on at least the basic livery colour. In the days before I possessed an airbrush, I used to select the most appropriate shade of car cellulose in an aerosol, and use this for the basic application of livery, going over to brushes and Humbrol for secondary livery colours, smokebox/footplate/cab roof and detail. Nowadays, Humbrol is available in aerosol form, which is a viable alternative, and the colour should at least be appropriate.

My own favoured approach is to airbrush on the main colour in cellulose, and to use enamels for everything else — detail painting, 'black' areas, lining and so on. I never bother to try and spray more than one colour, as I find the necessary masking up both tedious and liable to damage the base colour. I also tend to vary the shades of 'black' that I use for such areas as smokebox, footplate, cab roof, tender-top and chassis. And all those will be different from 'livery black'. Use of different paint types for primary and secondary colours also means that errors at the later stages can be expunged with a tissue and a spot of the appropriate thinners without damaging the base coat, provided the 'hardest' paint goes on first. Enamel thinners (use turps substitute) won't hurt dry cellulose, but cellulose thinners will strip enamel as effectively as Nitromors! Cellulose will also dry to very hard gloss, which is an ideal surface on which to rule lining and apply transfers. The final 'finish' is all determined at the varnish stage.

SPRAYING

These days, the normal way to paint models is by using an airbrush. More confusion surrounds these, but so far as we are concerned, what we require is an efficient miniature spray-gun. Many of the more expensive and sophisticated airbrushes are wasted on model work — at least, on the loco-painting side of it — as they are capable of a number of sophisticated and accurate functions which have no relevance to the successful application of a smooth, thin, even and dense layer of paint. If your only use for an airbrush is to paint locos and stock, don't waste your money on a high-falutin' graphics brush. A basic airbrush of good quality will do all that we ask. It is not my intention to delve deeply into the mechanics of airbrush design, but of the more basic types, the Paasche F1 or F3, the Badger 200 series and the DeVilbiss 'Sprite' are all suitable for loco painting. The Paasche, in particular, is a simple, rugged, easily-maintained outside-mix single action brush which gives good results. (Outside-mix brushes mix the paint and airstream 'in the open', as a last stage, rather

than passing an air-paint mix through the internals of the airbrush. Single action implies that only the air supply can be regulated; double-action brushes regulate both air and paint supplies.) I now possess both types of airbrush, but I tend to use the simpler Paasche most of the time as it is so easy to clean.

There is much discussion of the merits of compressors versus air from cans, but so long as an adequate supply at a suitable pressure is obtained, it doesn't matter that much. Mike Doherty painted quite a few of Pendon's coaches with a Badger 200 running off a tyre under the bench, which had the equivalent of a slow puncture. Every now and then, he'd lug it down to the garage for re-inflation . . . The disadvantage of 'stored air' is that as it runs down, the pressure drops off. If the reservoir is large enough, as in Mike's tyre, then the pressure drop over even quite a lengthy spraying bout will not be significant. Small cans of gas are more prone to losing their puff more rapidly, as well as being expensive. The ideal is a compressor charging a reservoir, with a proper pressure-regulating valve on the output, but this is an expensive toy not really justified for our occasional usage. Probably the best overall compromise is the small compressor, which gives a reasonably consistent, if rather 'pulsed' output. It is a good purchase for a club or modelling group.

The other essential, in my experience, is some form of moisture trap in the airline to the brush, as if you're not careful you'll find droplets of water condensing out as the air loses pressure from the compressor output or reservoir. These little droplets can play merry hell with the finish, causing the paint to 'splat' and blob with dire results. This is where the cans of gas are an advantage, as you're actually spraying with water-free Freon vapour rather than squashed atmosphere. With compressors, I reckon traps are a must. Either that, or move to the Sahara. . . .

SPRAYING BOOTH

This last item to be considered before we actually start applying paint is the provision of some form of spray booth. The function of this is to contain overspray and drift, and to protect the model from descending dust whilst the paint is in the initial drying stages. A cardboard carton on its side will serve quite well, although the ideal will also incorporate a fume extraction system. However, with the very small quantities of paint and thinners that we are using to paint our model (no more than about 5 cc for the average loco) fumes are not too much of a problem, so long as you are working in a well-ventilated space. But remember that finely divided thinners — enamel as well as cellulose — are a substantial fire hazard if allowed to collect, so do ensure that you are venting these, preferably to the great outside (open the window!) and don't smoke. For the same reason, avoid using a fan with a non-flameproof motor for extraction purposes. To keep paint droplets out of your lungs, a gauze mask of the 'Martindale' variety is an excellent safeguard.

A useful refinement in our spray booth is some means of turning the model in respect to the direction of spraying. My own solution is a cake-icing turntable (jumble sale, 50p) but a simple tray anchored to a block of wood with a screw will serve as well. I also find a selection of blocks of wood on which to prop the various bits of the model useful, while our old friend the blob of Blu-tak can also be used to hold things in place while the airbrush does its stuff.

PAINT CONSISTENCY

The next job is to mix our paint to a suitable spraying consistency. There is no hard-and-fast rule here, as the right degree of thinning will depend on a lot of factors, such as the type of paint, spray pressure, and the desired finish. Note this last, it is a very significant point. There is, fundamentally, no chemical difference between a matt paint and a gloss one. The difference lies in the manner in which they reflect light, which in turn is determined by the particle size in the finished surface. A matt paint has large particles giving a 'grainy' surface, and tends to reflect light haphazardly, whereas the gloss paint has finer particles, a relatively smooth surface, and tends to reflect the light consistently, giving the characteristic highlights of a shiny surface (the sketch should make this a bit clearer).

However, a moment's thought will reveal the potential risk with spraying — that the paint, finely atomized as it is, will dry 'on contact' as a series of small grains, rather than flowing to form a smooth surface. It is possible to vary the finish from near-matt to full gloss simply by altering the dilution of the paint, and the distance from which we spray. Hence, it is possible to spray from too far away, or with slightly too dry a mix, and end up with a matt finish when what we want is a high gloss. Why do we want a high gloss? It all comes back to the nature of the surface. The granular matt surface is obviously much less likely to take fine, clean lining than the smooth, hard, gloss. Imagine writing with a fountain-pen on hard vellum paper — and sandpaper. There is no need to ponder long over the comparative results! For the same reason, the matt surface does not take transfers (of any type, but especially waterslide) as well as a smooth gloss.

To achieve our smooth gloss, we need to dilute our paint to the point where it will flow together on the model, but not run. Cellulose paints generally have more finely-ground pigments than many enamels and this, coupled with the lower viscosity of the cellulose base compared with oil, means that they flow more easily, hence my preference. The only way to achieve the correct ratio of paint-to-thinners is to experiment by spraying test objects (tobacco tins and empty film canisters) and jug-

MATT AND GLOSS PAINTS

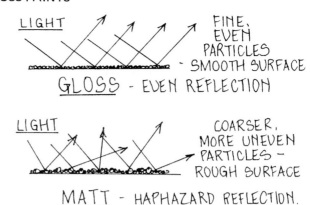

gling the dilution as you go. This is why I prefer the Paasche airbrush with its open cup, which facilitates the addition of more paint (on a brush) or more thinners (in the dropper). It is also good practice in using the airbrush, and I always like to 'warm-up' by spraying a few tests before I cut loose on the actual loco. The test pieces, by-the-by, are also useful for colour-checking and to practise lining-out on.

SPRAYING

Right. We now have the paint diluted to a suitable consistency, and enough of it to paint our model in the cup (few are the 4 mm locos you won't paint with a cupful). A last burst on the test object, and we can take a deep breath and start on the model. The golden rule is to make single passes, and to start and stop the airbrush off the model. I usually spray from left to right, and I resist the temptation to swing the brush to and fro — the point where you 'turn-round' will get a lot too much paint if you're not careful (or lucky). Some surfaces need vertical passes, and I like to work fairly close to the model — adjusting my paint mix and air pressure to suit. I concentrate on getting a nice even coat of the livery colour on those areas where it will show, and I tend to ignore any areas that will be overpainted in other colours. I could write reams on the trials and tribulations of spraying models, but this isn't the place for such a dissertation. The only way to obtain satisfactory results is to experiment until you get the hang of things.

If the worst happens, and the paint either runs or goes on too thick, then all is not lost. A dunk in a bath of thinners will remove the offending paint although I'm afraid it'll also take the primer and the knife stopping with it. Better the loss of a few hours' work, though, than a treacly paint job and the resultant dissatisfaction with the whole loco. Once a satisfactory base-coat is achieved, however, you can breathe a large sigh of relief. From now on, all but the most grievous of errors can be put right without impairing the fundamental

paint job. So pop the model under the drying cover, and put it in a nice warm spot while you put your feet up with a large gin to sooth the jangling nerves. (But clean the airbrush out first while you can still see straight!)

One last point in relation to spray painting, and that is the masking of components that do not need painting at all. After all, there is little point in carefully replacing appropriate components with brass or copper if you then obscure them with layers of primer and paint! Where the brass takes the form of a beading or spectacle rim—i.e., a raised surface—then I don't usually bother, preferring to scrape the unwanted paint off with a sharp knife or scraper once it is dry. Or it can be gently rubbed off with fine wet-and-dry on a rubbing stick. Bigger burnished fittings can either be made separate, as suggested at the start of this essay, or they may be cleaned by scraping, or by the judicious use of a Q-tip cotton-wool bud soaked in thinners. But don't miss . . . This still leaves some fittings in need of masking, which I do with metal polish. Brasso, used nice and thick (dredge up some gunge from the bottom of the tin) and applied to items such as boiler clacks, lubricators and whistles with a small paintbrush, then left to dry, forms a nice protective shield over the metal that will flake off readily once the spraying is completed, taking the unwanted paint with it.

BRUSH PAINTING

Time was, and not so long since, either, when there were few airbrushes outside graphic studios, and it was all down to the use of a paintbrush. It is possible to obtain a pretty good finish with a brush, and as previously remarked, I still resort to the hair of the sable for all my secondary painting. But hair of the sable it must be, for this is one operation in which the quality of the tool is paramount. No way will you get a good finish with the brush nicked out of junior's ninepenny paintbox from Woolworths. Having said that, it is not necessary to go right to the other extreme, and fork out a King's ransom on top-quality artists' watercolour sables. As with the airbrush, what we need is a straightforward good-quality brush which will hold and apply paint evenly and consistently. I have found that the Rowney Series 34 Student Sable serves as a good basis, moving up to the rather better Series 40 for the small sizes used for lining and lettering, or painting fine detail. There are equivalents in the Winsor & Newton range, and I daresay others, but sable-hair is superior to all else including synthetics, so accept no substitutes.

The best brush in the world will deteriorate rapidly if not loved, so look after the little darlings like your old granny. Wash them thoroughly in thinners (or MEK, very good for eliminating enamels), then in warm soapy water. Twizzle 'em to a point, and put the protective sleeve back on when not in use. Store them head-up in a pot, and try not to ever spread the bristles too wide. Treated like this, good sables will last for years, and give the best possible results.

The most suitable size and shape of brush is the subject of considerable debate, but there is no doubt that flat sables about ¼ in wide are jolly good for painting large, open areas such as boilers, tank sides or tenders. Avoid wash brushes, though; they have too much 'give' in the bristles. For the smaller, fiddlier areas, I use about a No. 3 pointed brush, while for detail work a No. 1 is about right. Fine work is, of course, the province of 0 or 00 brushes, and I believe there's even a 000 in the Series 40 range. My own armoury comprises a ¼ in flat watercolour sable (Winsor and Newton), a No. 1 and a No. 3 ordinary student sable (Rowney series 34) and a couple of No. 00 sables (Rowney series 40). Total

investment was about £10 and worth every penny.

As with spraying, the paint consistency must be right for successful brush painting. The desired dilution is often likened to single cream, which I think says it all. However, as with the airbrush, experiment upon a test object (which should, of course, have been primed in the same way as the model) will help establish the correct brew. I have found that, for model work, the Humbrol type of enamel is the easiest material to work with.

Conventional wisdom makes much of the thorough stirring of the tin of paint. That advice probably originates with the paint manufacturers, for once you thoroughly mix the contents of a tinlet, it starts an inexorable process of deterioration. How many half-used tinlets have you thrown away? The secret is to dip out the pigment and the varnish base separately, and mix them in some suitable container. I use those little pots that milk, cream, jam and butter arrive in at most catering outlets. This has two advantages; one can control the density of the paint, avoiding the overtranslucence that can result from the standard 'proportions as in the tin' mix; and the worst that can happen to the paint remaining in the tinlet is that an easily removed skin will form on the top of the upper, varnish layer of the contents.

The actual application of the paint is a pleasure. Work with smooth, flowing strokes, making sure that the brush does not get too 'dry' and overlapping to ensure even and complete coverage. I find it pays to work quickly and with the biggest practicable brush, so as to get all the paint on while it is still fluid.

It is possible, by the by, to attempt a limited amount of 'thermal re-flow' with enamels; if held in front of a radiant heat-source such as an electric fire and gently rotated, the paint will soften slightly and smooth itself out, effectively losing any brushmarks. The aim, as always, is to get good cover with the thinnest possible coat of paint — for paint is the enemy of detail, especially in the smaller scales. Do avoid any temptation to over-brush once the paint has started to 'skin', which, even with Humbrol, doesn't take long — hence the need for speed. My good friend Mike Sharman, a confirmed wielder of the brush, got into bother the first time he tackled a 7 mm loco, with its larger volumes and greater surface area — the speed of the paint-curing defeated him, and he was unable to get all the paint on fast enough for it to 'flow' and eliminate over-brushing marks.

Cellulose can be brushed as well (hence, 'Brushing Belco'), but it dries faster so is a lot trickier. The intention is to get a smooth surface by rubbing down — not easy on a small-scale model locomotive as it is on a motor-car. My advice is stick to enamels and make absolutely sure you let 'em dry properly — at least 36 hours in a warm, dry place with the cover on.

I have had considerable success with brushpainting, and for a small loco with an intricate livery — a Brighton 'Terrier', for instance — I'd still prefer to brush on all but the primer. Certainly, for all secondary colours and detail work, I would consider no other method. But that is the province of the next chapter.

My BR 'J67' was sprayed with matt black cellulose from an aerosol can (ozone friendly!), with all the detail work carried out in brushed enamels.

Here is the completed 'guinea-pig' model, BR N7/2 No. 69689, as running about 1955. This Finecast kit has had all the refining detailing and finishing techniques outlined in this book applied to it. The result is a model which hopefully transcends its origins.

CHAPTER EIGHT
THE FINAL FINISH

One of the best-finished whitemetal locos I have seen —
Peter Swift's wonderfully convincing Drummond 4—4—0 in post-war Southern livery.

SECONDARY COLOURS

Once the basic livery colour has been applied and cured, we enter the rewarding realms of detail painting, where it seems as if each additional colour and stroke of the brush adds life and versimilitude to our model. Smoke-boxes, footplating, valancing, bufferbeams, cab interiors, drag beams, cab roofs, sand-boxes, toolboxes and minor fittings can all receive their appropriate colours, which, if we look at the prototype with our seeing eye, will be a deal more subtle than the paintmakers would have us believe.

BLACK

The one colour that I never use unrelieved upon my locomotives is black. There is nothing to touch neat matt black for its ability to 'kill' a model stone dead, unless it's neat gloss black! In nature, true black is almost unknown — most 'black' is dark grey, dark brown or blue. What we actually need is a range of dark shades approaching black, but modified always to sug-gest the true perceived colour of the prototype. This is why I always contend that an unlined all-black loco is no sinecure. The smokebox needs to be a warm, graphite-grey, the foot-plate a dark slaty blue-brown, the chassis an oilier, yellower shade, and so on. My usual mixes are: smokebox, matt black, a dollop of silver, or 'oily steel' and a good dash of red oxide; footplate, Humbrol 145 'Dirty black' with a touch of grey and a stronger hint of track colour; and chassis, track colour with a stronger hint still of matt black and a touch of silver.

It certainly pays to experiment with mixing colours, and even varying the precise shades from engine to engine, to suggest differing shop dates and degrees of 'in service' deterior-ation. The same goes for buffer-beam ver-milion, a very variable hue, based on 'signal red' but often modified; reds tend to fade, and some engines long out of shops had buffer-beams that had reneged almost to a blushing pink. And don't forget that the buffer-beam was very much exposed to track dirt, particu-larly the rear-of-tender plank that was sullied by the wheels of the adjoining rolling-stock.

I also like to vary the shades of black on detail fittings such as lubricators and sandbox fillers, in an effort to suggest the differing func-tions of these components. Likewise, the cab roof, washed at will by the unremitting rains, will be an altogether different colour to the tender underframes, down among the dirt and dust of the permanent way. I personally find this sort of attention to the minutiae of colour-ing most rewarding, both in the execution, and in the final effect produced.

CHASSIS PAINTING

There are a number of approaches to the tick-lish problem of painting the chassis. The most logical method is to paint the mainframes at an early stage, before they are encumbered with wheels, cylinders, brake gear and so on. Provided that due provision is made for the attachment of post-painting detail, I have found this method most successful, particularly where the frames are a difference colour from the wheels; the 'H' class, for instance, was tackled in this way.

There was also less chance of paint getting into the 'works' if it is applied before the more delicate mechanical aspects of the chassis are commenced. The drawback is that much greater care is needed during the balance of the constructional process to avoid damaging the paintwork. I always use cellulose matt black as a basis for chassis (unless, like the 'H' or many GW locos, the frames are red oxide or brown, when I use red oxide primer), sprayed on from an aerosol can exactly as des-cribed for the grey primer. The chassis needs to be clean, and I warm it as well to ensure rapid paint drying and good adhesion. The matt black I use — 'Duplicolour' — is actually quite a 'soft' shade, and I also use it as 'livery black' on all-black locos (except LNWR). It needs only a modicum of 'letting-down' at the var-nish stage to give a convincing effect. On chas-sis, I brush a light coat of the 'chassis mix' over the basic black. The whole issue is then left to dry for a good long time, to ensure that the paint is hard.

Wheels are the very devil to paint. Again, this is an operation often better accomplished before the coupling rods and/or valve gear are finally fitted. I slip a scrap of paper between wheel and frame, and use an old brush that is no longer up to first-class work, as spokes are death to the point of any paint-brush. Or I may airbrush the wheels at the same time as the rest of the loco, if they are in the prime livery colour. Don't forget to fit the balance weights and boss overlays (if any) before paint-ing the wheels. A bit of Plasticine in the slots of Romford axle-nuts does much to alleviate the toy-like aspect of these wheels. It can easily be dug out if the wheels ever need to come off, and it takes paint quite well.

The alternative approach to chassis painting is simply to spray the whole issue once it is complete, and to remove the unwanted paint from wheelrims, rods, collectors and so on once it is dry. Do ensure that you rotate the wheels during the spraying process, or you will stencil the spoke-pattern on the frames. Oiling rotating joints before painting will stop the working aspects of the chassis being impaired, and I have successfully painted chassis 'under power', which made sure that (a) nothing got gummed up and (b) that the frames were not 'shaded' by the spokes at any point. Do make sure that you protect the motor from spray, both direct and 'drift'. This approach really only pays dividends on an all-black chassis, and I still like to differentiate the wheels from

such as outside frames, valances, splasher-fronts and so on. In these instances, there is normally a nice break-of-surface to help produce accurate edges, and the work is readily accomplished with a brush. Where the colours do meet on a panel, the joining edge can either be ruled, as described for borders, or it can be masked. In the fine work involved on model locomotives, ordinary motor-trade type mask-

TRANSFERS

These are probably the best method for most of us, and at best can give very good results indeed, if usually a trifle overscale. I do not like dry-print, however. It suffers from a definite 'shelf-life', and once it has gone off, it does the most peculiar things, none of them conducive to a good job on the model. If you need to use it, make sure you have a fresh

A good example of a professional lining job — neat, crisp work on Alan Ketley's Southern Mogul by Les Richards.

the frames with a little gentle brush-weathering.

Careful painting of chassis details can add life. Brake-blocks tended to get very hot, so lost their paint and rusted. Likewise, ashpan sides were often rusty, while around injectors and feed-pipes, water-marks, rust-streaks or limescale could all occur. Again, observation, a light touch, and subtle colours will give realistic results. Locomotive chassis, especially in the later days of steam, were often several degrees grimier than the more obvious and accessible upperworks of the locomotive. And don't overlook the effects of continuous lubrication, which impart an oily sheen to most chassis components, particularly the rods and valve gear. Parts of the chassis could be a good deal shinier than the superstructure!

LIVERY COLOURS

The other secondary painting job that often rears its head is that of applying a second — or even third — livery colour. The most common instance is the border, where the basic livery is panelled in a darker or contrasting shade. Invariably, the actual junction of the border with the main panel is lined, so this will help to overcome a less-than-dead-true edge. To get really accurate borders, however, it is best to rule the inner boundary of the border colour with a ruling pen, and fill in the rest by brush. This really takes the border into the realms of lining rather than painting, and it will be discussed in greater detail under that heading.

There are liveries, such as the pre-1906 Great Western, where the secondary livery colour was used on certain parts of the engine,

ing tape does not produce anything like a 'clean' enough edge. The best tape for our purpose is low-tack freezer bag sealing tape. This is usually red, but make sure it's the low-tack version, otherwise you can easily end up taking off the base colour when you peel back the mask.

LINING

Ah yes, lining. The *bête noire* of many a loco-modeller, and the ruination of many a fair model, the application of neat, square lining is rightly deemed one of the trickier aspects of the craft. Life is not too bad when it is merely a matter of a single line on a colour — LNER or LMS black-with-red mixed traffic livery, perchance. Things get a little more critical when the single line divides two colours, as in the GE blue livery, but are still quite manageable. Matters are a good deal trickier with the common 'two thin coloured lines each side of a black centre line'; and when one contemplates the full panoply of painted pomp entailed by a fully dressed LBSC or SECR loco, the heart does sink somewhat . . . .

There are, basically, only two methods of lining small-scale model locomotives; one may employ some sort of transfer, or one may work direct on the model with suitable paint applied by means of pens and brushes of one sort or another. I tend to discount various of the more esoteric methods dreamed up from time-to time by the more imaginative of the modelling fraternity, such as 'scratching through' or even inlaying the lining. There's quite enough scope for making a pig's ear of it with simple methods.

sheet, and that it hasn't been sitting in the model shop since the ark landed. No, for lining, water-slide is the best, especially if used in conjunction with a decal-setting fluid such as 'Solvaset' (see suppliers index). SMS and Kemco have good ranges of transfers, which, applied to our gloss surface, are easy to adjust, lie very flat and stay put.

It is also possible to line a complete loco with custom-made transfers, by executing the work panel-by-panel onto decal film. The *Model Railway Journal* project 'H' class tank was lined thus, and a full account appeared in issue 4. The great advantage with this approach is that one is working 'flat' on the bench, and that any mistakes made cannot affect the finish of the loco. One gets a number of 'shots' at the problem, and it is without doubt the best way of tackling the really complex liveries such as the full Wainwright SECR scheme on the 'H'.

PEN LINING

This is the most commonly-used approach to hand-lining models, and there is no doubt that some people acquire remarkable proficiency in this somewhat specialised art. Would I were one of them! However, where one has made an apt choice of painting materials, it is possible to produce acceptable results by a process of rule - trim - join - oops! - remove - try - again. Half the battle is having the right implement, the rest is down to getting the paint mix 'just so', having a reasonably steady hand, a supply of dodges and bodges — and luck!

None of these is quite as straightforward as I make it sound. Firstly, the implement that suits one man is anathema to another, and the

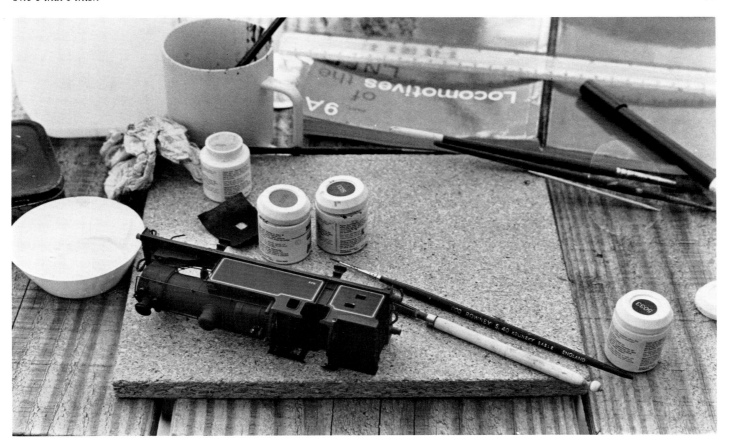

Lining essentials: good light (I was working in the garden), acrylic paints, ruling pen, good 00 sable, cocktail stick, mixing pots, and prototype reference.

only way to find out which sort of pen will give the best results in your own fist is to try them all. So what are the alternatives?

PENS

Easiest to use is the most recent type of draughting pen, the 'tube and needle' type, usually by 'Rotring'. The snag is that these pens will only work with special inks, most of which are too translucent for lining models. The black, however, is fine, and is invaluable for our purposes. There is also a Pelikan opaque white which many people swear by, and for those with black/white lining, this combination is hard to beat.

There are several versions of these pens, with the Staedler 'Mars' series and the Rotring 'Rapidograph' or the newer (and better) 'Isograph' being the most common. They are non-adjustable, and are classified by width of line drawn, in fractions of a millimetre. I find an Isograph .018mm plus Pelikan ink gives superb fine white lines, with an .025 or .035 for the black. These pens are not cheap, though—£7–£8 each—and need careful cleaning and storage.

Next in line, and quite a bit cheaper, are the Rotring 'Graphos' pens. These are in effect pre-set miniature bow-pens fitted with nib and internal reservoirs and they can be used with enamel paints such as Humbrol or with

designers colours, acrylics and synthetics. The pre-set nibs are again classified by width of line drawn, and are interchangeable. They are easy to clean so long as you forget about the internal reservoir system — which only works with inks — and load the pen-blades with a brush, as for an ordinary bow pen. Graphos pens can give very good results indeed, but they do need patience as the length of line that can be drawn with one 'fill' of paint is quite limited. Enamel paint in small quantities also changes consistency very quickly as the thinner evaporates, so frequent adjustments need to be made to keep the paint flowing smoothly. Several of the very best painters, such as Mike Doherty of Cavalier Coaches, swear by Graphos, with results that speak for themselves. The rest of us just swear at them, although at around £5 for the pen and £1.50 or so for the nibs the blasphemy is tempered by the economy. . . .

The old standby is the draughtsman's bow-pen, which is similar in principle to the Graphos but a lot heftier, and is fully adjustable. A good bow-pen in skilled hands will probably draw the finest line of the lot, and can take enough paint to produce a long line at one pass. But it needs to be a good pen, which will cost the wrong side of £10. British Thornton make some beauties, and there's a carbon-fibre version that is a real dream if you can run to it.

My own trusted bow-pen is an antique specimen with an ivory handle and steel bows that cost me £1 in a junk-shop in Marlborough many years since. It has very long bows of very good steel, and, since I replaced the rather coarse adjuster screw with one of 12BA, I find I can crank it right down to give a really fine line. I keep it clean and bright and sharpen the tips of the bows on a fine stone — not too much, or it digs in.

There is one last alternative, not often used these days, and that is the old-fashioned steel-nib mapping pen. Lofty Adcocks, who has rated previous mentions in these pages, and who could paint a loco with the best of them, was a devotee of the mapping pen. I find it very valuable for lining small components such as toolboxes, sandboxes, buffer-beams and splashers.

Of course, pens alone are not a complete answer to lining. The inevitable curved corners are best executed with a small brush of good quality — our No.00 series 40 sable. We also need straight-edges, curve templates, another small, clean brush for the removal of errors, tissues, Blu-tak and a cocktail stick or sharpened match for 'trimming'. I use a small clear plastic 60° set-square as a straightedge, as it helps to ensure that alignments are accurate and verticals vertical.

LINING PROCEDURE

Firstly—work in a good light, preferably daylight or colour-balanced fluorescent. It's less of a strain on the starting orbs. Lay the model on its side on a pad of soft material that is held in place on the bench. Lining's tricky enough without chasing the dratted model all over the table! I use kitchen towel, taped down with masking tape.

Next job is to mix the lining medium — paint or ink. Humbrol is one choice, but I've had good results with designers colour, both gouache and acrylic, which is water-thinned. I mix my colour in a little catering butter-pat pot, using the dropper to carefully meter the water or thinners. The only way to determine the correct mix is to keep trying the brew in the pen on our famous 'test object' which, if you recollect, was painted at the same time as the model itself. I also find a little 'surface activation' helps, especially with the water-based paints. I use a tissue moistened with thinners for Humbrol or, for gouache, with water and the merest trace of soap, and merely wipe over the surface I wish to line.

Now for it! Position the straightedge on the model, keeping it in place with a couple of small blobs of de-activated Blu-tak. Load the pen — not too much at one go, or the paint will start going off before you've used it all up — and try a quick line on the test object, to check for paint-flow and line width. If all is well, take a deep breath, and draw the pen steadily over the model, with just enough lateral pressure to keep it following the straight edge. A light touch is vital — don't press on the pen or it will dig in, and the chances are the straightedge will move as well. Use your free hand to steady the model, and don't try and go too fast.

Don't worry at this stage about corners—just aim to rule rectangles, with gaps where the corners come. Chances are that the lines will thicken slightly at the start and lift-off point, but don't worry about that either. Just concentrate on ruling all the basic lines in the one colour, the tidying-up comes later. Double lines can be ruled at the same time, by varying the angle at which the pen follows the straightedge. I like to work steadily until I've got down all the straight lines on one side of the loco, vertical and horizontal. The brushwork will take care of corners and gaps.

This is all very well for the straight bits of lining, but what of those sweeping curves around the splashers, across the cab front, below the cab roof, at the tops of the tender sides? The answer is to produce ruling edges of appropriate shape — lining templates. I make mine of thick Plastikard, about 40 thou, and hold them in place with the Blu-tak. When working around a curve, the pen needs to be held more vertically than when drawing straight lines, but otherwise the procedure is just the same.

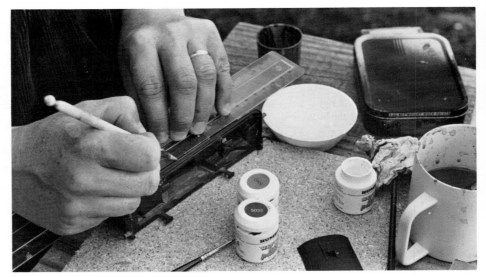

I start by ruling horizontals with the pen.

The verticals are then ruled in, leaving gaps at the corners . . . .

. . . . which are then touched in with the 00 sable brush.

The last stage of applying a lining colour is to use our 00 brush to touch in the corners and to join up any lines that don't quite meet. Because we only need to make very short strokes, it is surprisingly easy to get the brush to draw fine, accurate lines. As always, get your hand in on the test object, and do make sure the paint consistency is right. What suits the pen may be too thin for the brush.

ERRORS

All the above sounds nice and easy, but of course, life ain't like that, as we all know. Chances are, at least one line will blob, be out of square, in the wrong place, or die out where the pen ran dry ... The requirement is to remove the erroneous effort without disturbing the rest of the job. Our fine, clean brush with a drop of thinners will take the worst of the misplaced meridian away, but clean the brush on a lint-free cloth or tissue between strokes. Finish off with a tiny ball of tissue moistened in thinners and gripped in tweezers, or whizz into the nursery and steal a Q-tip from the baby.

The essential thing when removing mistakes is not to be in too much of a hurry, and to control the quantity of thinners on the surface. A succession of small erasures that each remove a fraction of the unwanted line is preferable to an attempt to scotch the lot at one go, which may erase more than you bargain for! Even after the last careful swabbing with tissue or Q-tip, there may still be a dull sheen of paint and thinner to mark the erstwhile course of the errant line. A piece of soft balsa sharpened to a chisel edge will polish that off *tout de suite*, and in any event such minor blemishes tend to disappear under the new lining and the varnish.

TRIMMING

Once all the lines are in their correct places, duly joined up, and the appropriate curves have been inscribed, there will still be a little tidying-up to do. Where a line has spread or blobbed slightly, a cocktail stick or sharpened match will 'rub-out' the unwanted portion of the line, and can be used (dry) along the straightedge or lining template. The No. 00 brush can also be used, with a tiny dip of thinners, to 'chivvy' edges, curves, blobs and corners. Where there is a double line with a black centre, I don't bother too much about the inside edges of the 'colour' lining, as the black will cover it anyway. Similarly, where the colour line separates a panel from a border, much can be done with a pen full of the border colour. This approach can also be used to produce super-thin lines, by a partial over-ruling of the coloured line to reduce its width.

What I never do is to start applying more basic livery colour to try and 'tidy-up' lining, as such additions always stick out like sore thumbs, and if the finish is cellulose or synthetic, there's a very real risk of disturbing the underlying paint. No, the whole system

Any blobbing, ragged edges or 'overshoots' can be removed with a cocktail stick.

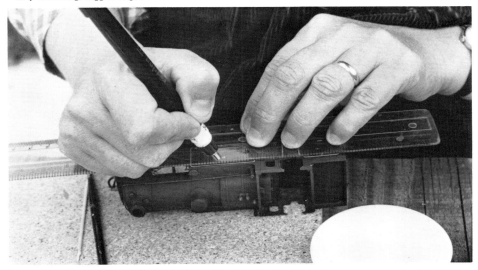

With the second colour similarly applied, a Rotring pen can be used to put on a centre 'black' line.

is based on the ability to remove unwanted lining without disturbing the main paint job, right down to the drastic expedient of wiping the slate clean and starting again! The only occasion in which I would contemplate covering excess lining colour is when a second lining or subsidiary livery colour can be used, as described for double-lines and borders. And that over-painting would certainly not be executed in paint with the same base as the main finish!

The application of second and subsequent lining colours is undertaken exactly as described, except that where this colour is black, I would always prefer the Rotring pen and Rotring black ink. The secret with the whole business is not to try and hurry, and as always throughout the whole loco-building process, not to accept first tries where these are second-best. The system does allow almost infinite adjustment, and you can always go back to basics and try again.

Once the 'panel lining' — that is, cabsides, valances, tender or tanksides, etc. — has been executed, I spray on a light coat of gloss var-

nish to protect it, before moving on to the next job, the re-fitting of the boiler bands.

BOILER BANDS

As previously remarked, boiler bands are thin, and at 4 mm and even 7 mm scales are best represented by paper or adhesive tape, rather than in the metalwork. I use either adhesive tape or thin bank paper, and in either case they are painted and lined flat on the bench, and stuck in place on the loco later. If I'm using paper, I 'stretch' it on a piece of thick card by dampening it, and gumming it down when wet with brown parcel tape. It can then be painted and lined as required once the paper has dried, when it will be flat and taut, and easy to work on. Once I've ruled up a sufficient supply of boiler bands — which includes a good few spares — I varnish the work and let it dry. (One sheet of boiler-band paper prepared thus will do umpteen locos).

The bands are cut out with a very sharp scalpel and a steel straightedge, and varnished on the back. Once the varnish has gone tacky,

Essentials for Rice's preferred Methfix transfers: transfer sheet, scalpel, tweezers, hypodermic, meths and water, and a clean brush. The hypodermic is used to ensure an accurate meths/water mix — it should be 3:1.

the bands may be manipulated into place with fine tweezers and the point of the scalpel. This isn't easy, but it's a darn sight easier than trying to paint bands *in situ*. The varnish should be enough to hold them in place, helped with a spot of UHU where the ends meet under the boiler. Once they're in place, a burst of varnish over the whole job will make all secure. Needless to say, this is yet one more job made a lot easier if the boiler falls off in your hand as a sub-assembly.

It is often necessary to pass the bands behind handrails, or to part them where pipework gets in the way. The eye is the best guide to getting them square, and to ensuring that the ends of the various sections line up. The varnish does allow a bit of adjustment so long as you don't press it down firmly until you're sure that all is in the right place. These boiler bands look very neat, and are worth the trouble even on an unlined black loco.

The transfer is cut out, and, with its backing tissue, peeled from the sheet. After dipping in the meths/water mix, the transfer is applied, positioned, and pressed down with a fingertip. It is then left for 10 minutes to set.

LETTERING AND HERALDRY

In a word — transfers. My own, very firm, preference is for PC Methfix, which I find truly excellent. If you use decals — sorry, waterslide transfers — be sure to cut as close to the outline of the characters as possible, and do use Decalset or Solvaset to get them to lie really snugly on the surface, particularly if there are rivets, cracks, edges or beadings at the transfer location. These setting agents also help to lose the otherwise prominent edges of the decal film.

With Methfix, most of these difficulties disappear. I still cut as close to the figure as I can, but this is mainly to ensure that the backing of one transfer does not interfere with the location of an adjoining or adjacent transfer.

Once the transfer is set, the backing tissue is soaked with clean water and gently eased away with a brush.

Otherwise, Methfix transfers just apply the character without any background film, in which respect they resemble dryprint types —but with the adjustability of the decal. Truly the best of both worlds!

With both decals and Methfix, the drill is to get the transfer onto the model, and to line it up once it is there. Provided you keep things wet until you've positioned everything to your satisfaction, there is infinite capacity for adjustment. With dryprint, it is necessary to position the lettering or number accurately before transferring it to the model. Any errors call for removal of the transfer — with all the risks that implies for the paintwork — and replacement. Dryprint, as already noted, definitely 'goes off', and I've had lettering literally falling off locos due to the glue failing. If you must use it, serve it up fresh each time.

VARNISHING

Once all the various stages of paint and decoration have, at long last, been completed and allowed to harden, the model requires a final coat of varnish to determine the degree of finish and the appropriate degree of 'toning down' of the colours. I use Humbrol gloss varnish, well-diluted with thinners and tinted with pale grey for most applications. The varnish is applied through the airbrush, and is drifted on at lowish pressure from about a foot away from the model. This gives a nice, silky semi-shiny sheen that looks just right for a 'clean but in service loco'. Moving the brush towards the model gives higher gloss, while pulling it back gives a duller finish. Likewise, darkening the grey tint of the varnish tends to dull the finish and subdue the colours, while adding more white keeps the colours fresh but prevents them from being too strident. There's infinite scope

The completed job — the N7's bunkerside lined and numbered. The 'RA5' route availability code was hand-lettered with the 00 brush.

for adjustment, and if you apply caution and start with a trace of tint, the required degree of finish can be built up in stages.

And now the hardest part of the whole process, almost impossible to achieve; leave the whole thing under the tin in a warm place to dry for at least 24 hours! Well, that's the ideal. I varnish last thing at night and trust to a good night's sleep to give the varnish a chance!

FINISHING TOUCHES

Once the varnish is hard, there remain but a few trifling jobs to complete the model. If sprung buffers have been substituted for cast-

ings, the heads will now need to be installed—place a drop of oil in the buffer-housings to combat corrosion which can easily afflict the springs. Screw couplings are also best fitted at this juncture — paint and varnish tend to stiffen them up to an unacceptable level, preventing them from hanging naturally.

Cab glazing needs to go in now, plus, of course, a crew. And please, no balletic firemen in frozen pirouette with a shovelful of coal 'twixt loco and tender . . . a terrible and unrealistic modelling cliché. Aim for figures in repose — my drivers lean nonchalantly over the cab sheets, while their firemen rest wearily

The cab windows are flush-glazed with 1/16in perspex, cut to fit using a paper template. It's easier if you remember to cut out these glazing pieces when the kit is still flat on the bench, unassembled. Glazing was held in place with thick cyano.

on their shovels. And if you've got a fireman, he'll need some coal in the tender on which to work his art . . .

Locomotive headlamps are another vital touch often overlooked. No locomotive ever ventured onto the metals outside the limits of the depot without displaying the appropriate lamp or combination of lamps to describe the nature of the movement of traffic. The standard code of headlamps is shown in my diagram, and this pertained generally from the 1923 grouping, although there were local variations and additions, while some lines also used head-code discs, destination boards, reporting numbers or semaphore indicators to give more comprehensive train descriptions. Pre-grouping practice was much more divergent, and will be a case for study.

Top: With all the detail in place and the chassis painted, it's time for a little weathering. Prototype reference is a good idea. I used dry-brushed acrylic paint, very sparingly, and Carr's weathering powders. I mix these to obtain a range of shades. On the nearside, the GE-pattern vacuum-operated push-pull gear is prominent. Note also the blanking plates on smokebox and sidetank, covering the holes left by removal of the condensing gear.

Centre: Another characteristic touch is the set of fire-irons parked atop the sidetank.

Left: Coal is essential. I crush up the real thing (put it in a thick polythene bag, and whop it with a hammer), and build a coal load into wet Uhu.

In 4 mm scale, there are some very nice model lamps available from firms like Kenline and Springside. These are pre-painted in the appropriate colours (no, they weren't all white), and are modelled on the various patterns in use by the 'Big Four' and BR. These lamps are fitted with 'brilliants', small jewels cut to give a sparkle, often a bit on the bright side but easily toned down a bit with a dab of tinted varnish. The trouble comes in the fixing; no problem on layouts where locomotives are permanently assigned to set duties, and can thus carry the appropriate headcode by means of lamps stuck in place with epoxy or cyano. But for those of us whose engines must perform

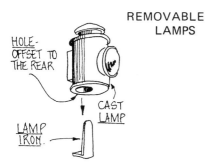

REMOVABLE LAMPS

HOLE - OFFSET TO THE REAR

CAST LAMP

LAMP IRON

a multitude of duties, then compromise is inevitable. We must either accept wrong headcodes, or provide demountable lamps. It can be done, although proper bracketry is very tricky at 4 mm scale. The usual dodge is to drill a hole into the base of the lamp, and sit it over the lamp-iron, rather than in front of, or beside, as the prototype case may be. 7 mm boys have the advantage of we small-scale fry here . . .

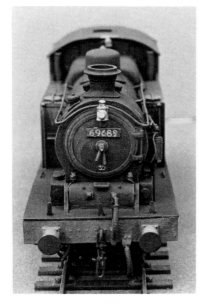

Head-on, the jewelled Kenline LNER-pattern lamp is most convincing, as is that lovely Exactoscale screw coupling. Buffer-beam hoses are my own lost-wax castings, and the number-plate is hand-lettered.

WEATHERING

The last job on any locomotive is weathering: we have already undertaken a certain amount in our use of colour and the detail touches applied to the chassis. But the superstructure? Often it is a job that doesn't get done at all, either because one can't bring oneself to sully painstaking finishing work, or possibly because the prototype itself was kept in top order. Weathering is, I fear, either grossly overdone, or not attempted; either is the enemy of realism. Nothing gives the game away more than a layout whose loco stud are immaculate to an engine, resplendent with copper caps, burnished brass and full lining where the prototype was unembellished. Unless, perhaps, it is the layout which looks like an animated rendition of Barry scrapyard — rust, grease, scale,

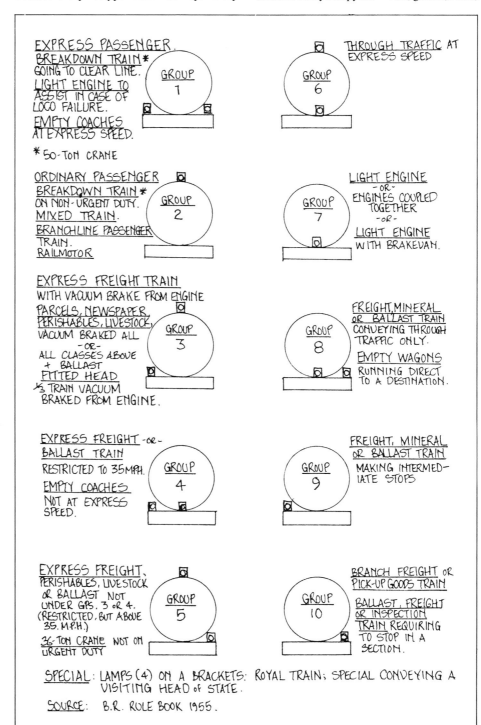

EXPRESS PASSENGER. BREAKDOWN TRAIN * GOING TO CLEAR LINE. LIGHT ENGINE TO ASSIST IN CASE OF LOCO FAILURE. EMPTY COACHES AT EXPRESS SPEED.
GROUP 1

* 50-TON CRANE

THROUGH TRAFFIC AT EXPRESS SPEED
GROUP 6

ORDINARY PASSENGER BREAKDOWN TRAIN * ON NON-URGENT DUTY. MIXED TRAIN. BRANCHLINE PASSENGER TRAIN. RAILMOTOR
GROUP 2

LIGHT ENGINE -OR- ENGINES COUPLED TOGETHER -OR- LIGHT ENGINE WITH BRAKEVAN.
GROUP 7

EXPRESS FREIGHT TRAIN WITH VACUUM BRAKE FROM ENGINE PARCELS, NEWSPAPER PERISHABLES, LIVESTOCK, VACUUM BRAKED ALL -OR- ALL CLASSES ABOVE + BALLAST FITTED HEAD ⅓ TRAIN VACUUM BRAKED FROM ENGINE.
GROUP 3

FREIGHT, MINERAL OR BALLAST TRAIN CONVEYING THROUGH TRAFFIC ONLY. EMPTY WAGONS RUNNING DIRECT TO A DESTINATION.
GROUP 8

EXPRESS FREIGHT -or- BALLAST TRAIN RESTRICTED TO 35 MPH. EMPTY COACHES NOT AT EXPRESS SPEED.
GROUP 4

FREIGHT, MINERAL OR BALLAST TRAIN MAKING INTERMEDIATE STOPS
GROUP 9

EXPRESS FREIGHT, PERISHABLES, LIVESTOCK OR BALLAST NOT UNDER GRS. 3 OR 4. (RESTRICTED, BUT ABOVE 35. M.P.H.) 36-TON CRANE NOT ON URGENT DUTY
GROUP 5

BRANCH FREIGHT OR PICK-UP GOODS TRAIN BALLAST, FREIGHT OR INSPECTION TRAIN REQUIRING TO STOP IN A SECTION.
GROUP 10

SPECIAL: LAMPS (4) ON A BRACKETS: ROYAL TRAIN; SPECIAL CONVEYING A VISITING HEAD of STATE.
SOURCE: B.R. RULE BOOK 1955.

failing paint and limestreaking are all to be found on locomotives 'in service', but not to the exclusion of all else!

As with all other aspects of finishing, subtlety and a degree of understatement give the most convincing results. I tend to limit weathering to traces and suggestions of grime, the merest hints of rust on wearing points, plus water-washing where there might be spillage, and if I do allow myself the occasional minor outbreak of limestreaking — only appropriate in hard water areas anyway — I restrict it severely to the odd leaking gland on a clack or live-steam feed. The photographs give some idea of the sort of thing that can be achieved.

All of which concludes the cosmetic aspects of building model locomotives from whitemetal kits.

TAILPIECE

In the two years and more that this book has been in the writing, a lot has happened in the field of whitemetal kit manufacturing. K's, those doughty pioneers, have disappeared, at least for the moment. Bob Wills has sold the 'Finecast' range, and several other well known ranges have changed hands. Several new manufacturers have entered the field, and DJH have continued to lift the 'top end' of the whitemetal kit market in both sophistication and price. Indeed, many of the latest kits render much of what I have written in these pages redundant, for they have answered my criticisms and anticipated my improvements! Alas, I can't afford to buy them, so must soldier on with the more accessible specimens still lurking in my workshop cupboard.

The range of complementary components available from the trade has also grown dramatically, with all sorts of etched and cast detailing packs, alternative mechanical and cosmetic components, or even kits-to-alter/ improve other kits! The choice is so bewildering one hardly knows where to start, but one thing is clear: it is now possible to produce a higher quality of model from a whitemetal kit than ever before. Some of the best builders, such as Alan Ketley, Chris Pendlenton or Alan Sibley, are turning out whitemetal models that can stand comparison with anything made anywhere.

For all these improvements, increased sophistication and greater choice, it is still the model built with that bit 'extra' in the way of care, dedication and uncompromising fidelity that shines through as being, in its completion, far more than the sum of the parts. There are still 'kitbuilt locomotives' and 'model locomotives built from kits'. It's worth aiming to make yours one of the latter.

A nose for a tailpiece. This study of Peter Swift's Drummond 'D15', built from an LSWR Models kit, encapsulates all that I aspire to in my kitbuilding endeavours — a 'model locomotive built from a kit'.